Roadside Trees and Shrubs of Oklahoma

D1568963

By Doyle McCoy

Keys to the Flowering Plants of Pontotoc County, Oklahoma (Ada, Oklahoma, 1963)

A Study of Flowering Plants (Lawton, Oklahoma, 1976)

Roadside Flowers of Oklahoma 2 vols. (Lawton, Oklahoma, 1976, 1978)

Roadside Wild Fruits of Oklahoma (Norman, Oklahoma, 1980)

To my wife, Pearl;
our daughter, Judy;
our son-in-law, Tony;
and our grandson, Allen

Library of Congress Cataloging-in-Publication Data

McCoy, Doyle, 1917–
  Roadside trees and shrubs of Oklahoma.

  Bibliography: p. 106.
  Includes index.
    1. Trees—Oklahoma—Identification. 2. Shrubs—Oklahoma—Identification. 3. Roadside flora—Oklahoma—Identification.   I. Title.
QK484.05M32   582.1609766   80–5944

ISBN: 0–8061–1556–4

2   3   4   5   6   7   8   9   10   11   12   13   14   15   16

Contents

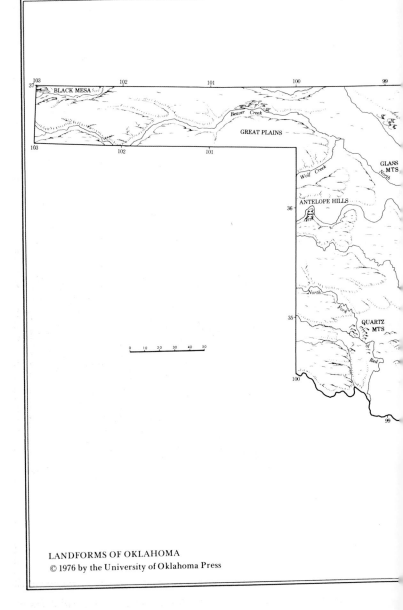

BLACK MESA

Beaver Creek

GREAT PLAINS

Wolf Creek

GLASS MTS.
North

ANTELOPE HILLS

North Fork

QUARTZ MTS

of

Red

0 10 20 30 40 50

LANDFORMS OF OKLAHOMA
© 1976 by the University of Oklahoma Press

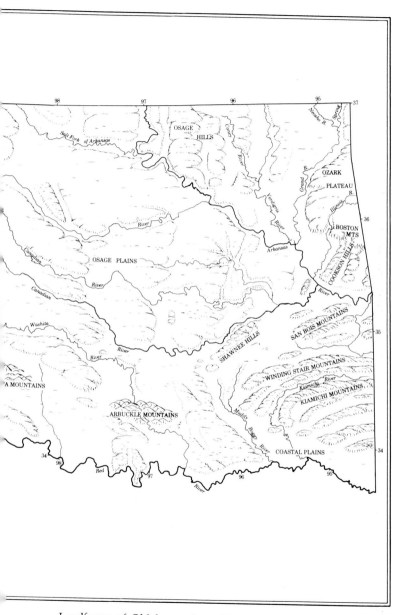

Landforms of Oklahoma, from Morris, et al., *Historical Atlas of Oklahoma.* © 1976 by the University of Oklahoma Press.

Illustrations

ix

x

Introduction

FOREWORD

When I became fully convinced that a book of this kind would help to acquaint Oklahomans with the great wealth of plantlife in our state, I was faced with the problem of deciding how extensive the coverage should be. I believe that the one hundred fifty-six different trees and shrubs that are included represent the best coverage possible. Most of them are widely distributed, while others have unique features to offer.

PURPOSE

This tree and shrub guide has been produced in response to requests for such a publication. The requests have come largely from the same individuals who have enjoyed my previous books, *Roadside Flowers of Oklahoma*, volumes 1 and 2, and *Roadside Wild Fruits of Oklahoma*. This book, like the flower guides and the fruit guide, emphasizes use of color plates for identifying Oklahoma's plants and provides a nontechnical description of them.

METHOD OF PREPARATION

I have made periodic visits to every Oklahoma county to photograph trees and shrubs. This has required much time and considerable study, but it has been a rewarding experience. Even though I have been a plantlife enthusiast and a trained botanist for many years, I have always found a few surprises on these visits. The education has been rewarding for me. It is exciting to share some of my knowledge and appreciation of these plants with others who are interested.

The photographs were made with a 35-mm camera equipped with a close-up lens. Usually a small branch, with its attached leaves, was arranged before a very dark background. Flowers or fruits were also included, when possible, for more conclusive identification. Several shots of each specimen were made so that some option could be used in choosing the one for a plate.

Additional information is provided for each plant so that it may be more conclusively identified and enjoyed. This information includes its description, its distribution in the state, and additional local or common names. The source of my information is threefold: (1) personal observations over many years, (2) discussions with other botanists and local residents, (3) published references that are listed in this book.

The sequence or organization used in this book is based on that of most botany books; thus, the gymnosperms appear first, followed by the angiosperms. This, of course, groups them by families as well.

I am indebted to many people from a broad segment of Oklahoma's citizenry. Special encouragement has come from members of the Oklahoma Academy of Science; members of the Oklahoma Garden Clubs; members of the Oklahoma Ornithological Society; fellow botanists in colleges, universities, and public schools; and owners who shared their acreages with me.

Roadside
Trees and Shrubs
of Oklahoma

MEXICAN CEDAR
Juniperus Ashei

Pine Family
Pinaceae

ONE-SEED JUNIPER
Juniperus monosperma

Pine Family
Pinaceae

RED CEDAR
Juniperus virginiana

Pine Family
Pinaceae

MEXICAN CEDAR

These small trees are also known as One-seed Juniper and Arbuckle White Cedar. They are most often shrublike, with several trunks growing from one base and forming an irregular or rounded head 8–25 feet high. The leaves are shorter and thicker than those of the Red Cedar. The fruits are about 1/3 inch in diameter, almost globular in shape, and contain one seed (rarely two seeds). The bark of the Mexican Cedar is grayish or black compared with the tan or brown bark of the Red Cedar. These small trees are mostly restricted to the Arbuckle and Wichita ranges of Oklahoma.

ONE-SEED JUNIPER

These small trees are also known as Cherrystone Juniper, West Texas Juniper, Redberry Juniper, and Sabina. They are freely branched and often shrubby when growing in sterile soils. The leaves are minute, grayish green, and overlapping on very small stems. The older stems are reddish brown. The fruiting cones are dark blue to brown, almost spherical, and 1/8–1/4 inch thick. In Oklahoma these trees are well established only in the western portion of Cimarron County, where they grow on the rocky slopes.

RED CEDAR

These trees are also known as Red Savin, Juniper, Carolina Cedar, Eastern Red Cedar, and Pencil Wood. They are usually 30 to 40 feet in height but may be much smaller or much larger, depending on the environment. Young trees have narrowly conical crowns, but in maturity they become irregular and round-topped. They are typically found in dry limestone soils or outcroppings of limestone hillsides and often invade old fields. The leaves are scalelike, ovate, and about 1/16 inch long. They are dark bluish green and persist on the twigs for five or six years. The fruits are about 1/4 inch in diameter, nearly globular, dark blue, and covered with a whitish film. They are consumed by several species of birds. These trees are widely distributed in Oklahoma.

SHORTLEAF PINE
Pinus echinata

Pine Family
Pinaceae

NUT PINE
Pinus edulis

Pine Family
Pinaceae

4

LOBLOLLY PINE
Pinus Taeda

Pine Family
Pinaceae

SHORTLEAF PINE

These trees are also known as Yellow Pine, Spruce Pine, Short-shot Pine, Bull Pine, Pitch Pine, Carolina Pine, Old-field Pine, and Rosemary Pine. They attain a height of 80 to 100 feet with a diameter of 2 to 3 feet. They seem to grow best in well-drained, sandy, or gravelly clay soils. They drop their lowermost branches early, even when they are not crowded, and produce tall, straight trunks. The crowns are mostly rounded, with long, slender branches. The leaves are needlelike and usually grow in bundles of two, though rarely in bundles of three or even four. They are 2–5 inches long, bluish green, and flexible. The cones are 1–2 inches long and ovate when mature. They require two years for maturation and persist on the twigs for a few years. These trees are restricted to the eastern one-fifth of Oklahoma but are found in abundance in most of that portion.

NUT PINE

These trees are also known as Piñon Pine and Colorado Pinyon Pine. They are small trees that have bushy tops and orange-colored branches. The leaves occur in clusters of two or, rarely, three. They are stiff, curved, dark green, and about one inch long. The fruiting cones are rounded, 1–2 inches broad, and produce large seeds. These seeds have been widely used as food by people, as well as by birds and small mammals. In Oklahoma these trees are found only in the Black Mesa of Cimarron County unless they have been transplanted.

LOBLOLLY PINE

These trees are also known as Old-field Pine, Yellow Pine, and Long-leaf Pine. They reach a height of 130 feet or more and may attain an age of 300 years in favorable habitats. The leaves are slender, stiff, slightly twisted, 3–8 inches long, and light blue green and grow in clusters of 2–3. The cones are 2–6 inches long when they mature and are armed with short, stout prickles. These trees are limited to the southeast corner of the state and are much less common there than are the Shortleaf Pines. They are mostly restricted to the lowlands.

CYPRESS
Taxodium distichum

Pine Family
Pinaceae

ERECT EPHEDRA
Ephedra antisyphilitica

Ephedra Family
Ephedraceae

GIANT CANE
Arundinaria gigantea

Grass Family
Gramineae

CYPRESS

These trees are also known as Bald Cypress, Swamp Cypress, Southern Cypress, and Tidewater Red Cypress. They often attain a height of 100–150 feet and a trunk diameter of 3–6 feet or possibly more. The peculiar root system produces irregular conical structures known as knees. They grow best in swamps, but do fairly well in well-drained soils of uplands. The leaves are ½–¾ inch long, linear, and arranged in featherlike rows on slender twigs that are shed in the fall. The fruiting cones are almost globular, ¾–1 inch wide and formed of hard scales. These trees are found in Oklahoma only in the southeastern section.

ERECT EPHEDRA

These shrubs are 1–3 feet tall and profusely branched. The branches are opposite or whorled at the stem nodes and are very rigid. The leaves are so small that they are usually overlooked. The male flowers are produced on separate plants from those of the female flowers. The fruits are single-seeded, oval, brown, and ¼–⅓ inch long. These small shrubs are found in the dry soils of gravelly plains, rocky slopes, old fields, and pastures. They are restricted to a very few southwestern Oklahoma counties.

GIANT CANE

These plants are also known as Southern Cane and Bamboo. They may reach a height of as much as 30 feet, with main stems that are as thick as an inch. The stems are woody, resulting in their shrubby character. The leaves are typical of the grass family, with their sheathing petioles and flattened, parallel-veined blades. Each blade of the primary stem is 5–12 inches long and 1–2 inches wide, but those of the smaller branchlets are much reduced in size. The flowers and fruits (grains) are borne in terminal racemes or simple panicles. These woody grasses spread from creeping rhizomes and thrive in low grounds or shallow waters of lakes and swamps in a few of Oklahoma's southeastern counties.

PALMETTO
Sabal minor

Palm Family
Palmaceae

COMMON GREENBRIER
Smilax Bona-nox

Lily Family
Liliaceae

8

WHITE POPLAR
Populus alba

Willow Family
Salicaceae

PALMETTO

These small shrubs are also known as Blue-stemmed Palmetto. They are dwarf palms with creeping, underground stems. The leaves are fan-shaped, nearly circular, and deeply cleft into many radiating divisions that are bluish green. These leaves are 1–2 feet broad and are mostly borne in small clusters, but occasionally occur singly. They grow in open woodlands or low floodplain meadows of Oklahoma's McCurtain County.

COMMON GREENBRIER

These plants are also known as Low Greenbrier. They have many branches from underground, woody rhizomes. These branches are mostly shrubby or, more rarely, climbing vines. They are armed with hooked spines. The leaves are heart-shaped, simple, alternate, and 1–5 inches long. Their margins are smooth or slightly supplied with slender prickles. The petioles are ¼–⅗ inch long. The fruits mature in September through November. They are globular, black berries that are about ¼ inch thick. These plants are the most widely distributed of Oklahoma's greenbriers, occurring in all but a few northwestern counties.

WHITE POPLAR

These trees are also known as Aspen, Dutch Beech, Silverleaf Poplar, and Whitebark Poplar. They are large trees with heights of 80–120 feet, trunk thicknesses of 4–6 feet, and light-gray bark. The leaves are alternate, simple, 2–4 inches long, and almost as broad. They have 3–5 lobes. They are silvery white beneath and dark green above. The petioles are long and slightly flattened. These trees have been used as landscape ornaments for many years and have become naturalized on a limited basis. They prefer rich, moist soils in open areas, but they tolerate many other habitats very well.

COTTONWOOD
Populus deltoides

Willow Family
Salicaceae

PEACHLEAF WILLOW
Salix amygdaloides

Willow Family
Salicaceae

SILVERLEAF WILLOW
Salix caroliniana

Willow Family
Salicaceae

COTTONWOOD

These trees are also known as Eastern Cottonwood, Poplar, Virginia Poplar, and Whitewood. They usually reach a height of 100 feet. They typically grow in the rich, moist soils of swamps, lake margins, or stream banks but will survive, when transplanted as saplings, in drier habitats. They have broad, open crowns and continuous tapering trunks and make good shade trees. Their branches are somewhat weak, which sometimes results in damage from wind or ice storms. The leaf blades of these trees are broadly triangular (deltoid) and 3–5 inches long. The marginal teeth are short, hooked, and tipped with glands. The petioles are about as long as the blades. These trees are widely distributed throughout Oklahoma.

PEACHLEAF WILLOW

These trees are 40–60 feet tall and have trunk diameters of 1–2 feet. The branches are long and slender, resulting in considerable drooping at the tips. The leaves are simple, alternate, ovate-lanceolate, 2–5 inches long, finely serrate, and light green. The petioles are ½–¾ inch long. The flowers are inconspicuous in long catkins (staminate and pistillate on separate trees). These are the only willows that are natives of the Rocky Mountains and are truly trees. They are distributed over all of Oklahoma except the far southeast. They seem to prefer sandy or gravelly hillsides or stream banks.

SILVERLEAF WILLOW

These small willows are also known as Ward's Willow and Gray Willow. They seldom reach a height of 30 feet. They are freely branched with either spreading or drooping lateral branches. The bark is dark brown. The leaves are alternate, simple, slightly serrate, light green above, and silvery beneath. Each leaf is 2–6 inches long, oblong-lanceolate, and ½–1½ inches broad. Like others of this family, the trees are either male or female. The capsules of the female trees are conic and smooth, and they mature in early summer. These small trees grow in low, moist areas of stream banks in many areas of southern or eastern Oklahoma.

SANDBAR WILLOW
Salix interior

Willow Family
Salicaceae

BLACK WILLOW
Salix nigra

Willow Family
Salicaceae

**SOUTHERN
WAX MYRTLE**
Myrica cerifera

Wax Myrtle Family
Myricaceae

SANDBAR WILLOW

These small trees are also known as Riverbank Willow, Longleaf Willow, Narrow-leaf Willow, Red Willow, White Willow, Osier Willow, and Shrub Willow. They are most often shrubby and form thickets. They are limited to moist soils along streams or near lakeshores. The leaves are simple, alternate, linear-lanceolate, toothed, and 2–4 inches long. The blades are green on both sides and differ from the Black Willow by the much smaller number of teeth on the margins. These shrubby trees are found only in the western portion of the state.

BLACK WILLOW

These trees are also known as Water Willow, Swamp Willow, Pussy Willow, and Scythe-leaved Willow. They are the largest of our native willows. They commonly reach a height of 30–50 feet when they grow in favorable environments along streams or in bottomlands. The crowns are likely to be irregular and are rounded at the top. The trunks are crooked, and they almost always occur in clumps of 3–5, which causes even more irregular growth. The leaves are narrowly lancelike with long, tapering tips. They are 3–6 inches long and finely toothed on their margins. Because their branches have very little strength, Black Willows are not popular landscape trees. These trees are widely distributed over Oklahoma but are more abundant in the southeast because of the moisture they require.

SOUTHERN WAX MYRTLE

These shrubs or small trees are also known as Waxberry, Candleberry, Bayberry, Spicebush, Sweet Oak, and Ta-low Shrub. They have very crooked branches and are mostly evergreen in habit. The leaves are simple, alternate, 2–5 inches long, ¼–¾ inch wide, and have scattered teeth on the margins of the upper half. The flowers are in catkins with male flowers and female flowers on separate plants. The fruits are bluish when mature, globose, very small, and mature in September or October. They occur infrequently in the low, moist woodlands of Oklahoma's southeastern counties.

PECAN
Carya illinoensis

Walnut Family
Juglandaceae

**SCALY-BARK
HICKORY**
Carya ovata

Walnut Family
Juglandaceae

14

BLACK HICKORY
Carya texana

Walnut Family
Juglandaceae

PECAN

These trees are also known as Illinois Nut and Soft-shell Hickory. They are among Oklahoma's most beautiful trees and are widely cultivated throughout the South as shade trees, as well as for the food supply from the nuts. They often attain a height of 100 feet or more and a trunk diameter of over 3 feet. They branch freely to form broad, rounded crowns. The leaves are alternate, pinnately compound, and have 11–17 leaflets. These leaflets are 4–7 inches long, pointed at the tips, and sharply toothed on the margins. The fruits are borne in small clusters. They are 1–2½ inches in length and oblong, and have thin, 4-winged husks. The nuts are light brown with hard shells and sweet kernels. These trees are widely distributed but are much more numerous in the eastern half of Oklahoma.

SCALY-BARK HICKORY

These trees are also known as Shagbark Hickory, Shellbark Hickory, and Upland Hickory. They may reach heights of 50–80 feet and mostly have oblong crowns. They reach their largest growth in bottomlands but are more frequently found on hillside slopes. The leaves are alternate and pinnately compound and contain 5–7 leaflets. The latter are oval, serrate, and 2–7 inches long. The fruits are globose or ellipsoidal nuts, 1–2 inches in diameter, with thick husk covers. These nuts are white to pale tan and have thin shells and sweet kernels. These trees are found in the eastern third of Oklahoma.

BLACK HICKORY

These trees are also known as Buckley Hickory, Texas Hickory, and Pignut Hickory. They are no more than 80 feet tall and have short, crooked branches. The leaves are alternate, and pinnately compound and usually have seven leaflets. Each leaflet is 4–6 inches long, oval to obovate, and serrate along the margins. The hulls of the nuts are globose and 1¼–2 inches in diameter. These trees grow on rocky hillsides or sandy uplands throughout the eastern half of the state.

MOCKERNUT HICKORY
Carya tomentosa

Walnut Family
Juglandaceae

BLACK WALNUT
Juglans nigra

Walnut Family
Juglandaceae

WESTERN WALNUT
Juglans rupestris

Walnut Family
Juglandaceae

MOCKERNUT HICKORY

These trees are also known as White-heart Hickory, Big-bud Hickory, Bullnut Hickory, and White Hickory. They often attain heights of 50–75 feet, with trunks that are 2–3 feet thick. They grow in a variety of habitats but seem to do best in rich, moist soils. The leaves are alternate and pinnately compound and contain 5–9 (usually 7) leaflets. Each leaflet is lanceolate to obovate and 2–7 inches long. They are finely serrate on the margins. The fruits are globose to obovoid, 1½–2 inches long, with thick shells and sweet kernels. These trees are limited to the easternmost one-sixth of Oklahoma.

BLACK WALNUT

These trees are also known as River Walnut. They are freely branched and 50–75 feet tall, with trunks that are 2–4 feet thick. They have open and rounded crowns. They attain maximum growth in bottomlands where deep, rich soils are available. They do not form thickets but rather seem to be interspersed with other hardwood trees. The leaves are alternate, pinnately compound, and 1–2 feet in length with 13–23 leaflets. The leaflets are 2–4 inches long with slender tips and sharply toothed margins. The fruits are globular and 1–2 inches thick, with semifleshy, nonsplitting husks. They mature in October, and most of them are dispersed within a month. These trees are widely distributed but are most frequent in the eastern half of Oklahoma.

WESTERN WALNUT

These trees are also known as Small Walnut, in reference to the size of their fruits. They are of medium size, reaching heights of 20–30 feet. The twigs have red brown hairs. The leaves are alternate, pinnately compound, and contain 12–23 leaflets. The latter are 2–3 inches long, lanceolate, serrate, and rounded at their bases. The fruits are nuts that are covered with thin husks which have red-brown hairs. Each nut is only ½–¾ inch in diameter and almost spherical in shape. These small walnut trees are found only in the western half of Oklahoma, where they thrive mostly along streams.

ALDER
Alnus maritima

Birch Family
Betulaceae

RIVER BIRCH
Betula nigra

Birch Family
Betulaceae

BLUE BEECH
Carpinus caroliniana

Birch Family
Betulaceae

ALDER

These trees are also known as Seaside Alder. They are small, slender trees with trunks about 4–6 inches thick and crowns that are rounded. They prefer margins of spring-fed streams in limestone soil. The leaves are alternate, obovate, narrowed at the base, finely serrate, and 2–4 inches long. They have short petioles. The dark-brown fruits are conelike, oval, about ½ inch long, and mature in August. They remain attached during the following winter. These small trees, which are essentially seaside trees, are found in a few locations in Oklahoma's Johnston and Pontotoc counties.

RIVER BIRCH

These trees are also known as Red Birch and Black Birch. They are usually about 30–50 feet tall with trunks 1–2 feet in diameter. They often separate near the base to form a few branches. These in turn have spreading to drooping branches, resulting in broad, irregular crowns. They are restricted to wet soils of lake margins, stream banks, or flooded lowlands. The leaves are ovate with short tips that are either pointed or blunt. The leaf margins are irregularly toothed. Each leaf blade is 1–3 inches long, dark green above, and yellow green below. They are alternately arranged on slender stems. The seeds are produced in conelike spikes that are 1–2 inches long. These trees are found throughout the eastern third of Oklahoma.

BLUE BEECH

These trees are also known as Water Beech, American Hornbeam, and Ironwood. They usually are small with a height of 10–30 feet and a trunk diameter of 8–12 inches. The trunks are typically short and crooked. The slender branches form a low, spreading crown. They thrive in deep, rich, wet soils and are encountered along streams or near springs. The leaves are simple, alternate, ovate, pointed at the tips, serrate, and 2–4 inches long. The fruits are peculiar and quite distinctive. They are small, ovoid nutlets that are enclosed in 3-lobed bracts. They are produced in pairs in loose, drooping clusters. These trees are distributed throughout the eastern half of Oklahoma.

AMERICAN FILBERT
Corylus americana

Birch Family
Betulaceae

IRONWOOD
Ostrya virginiana

Birch Family
Betulaceae

CHINQUAPIN
Castanea pumila

Beech Family
Fagaceae

AMERICAN FILBERT

These shrubs are also known as Hazelnut. They are 3–10 feet tall and form thickets in hedgerows or woods where rich, moist soils are available. The leaves are simple, alternate, 3–6 inches long, ovate, and have serrate margins. The petioles are about ¼ inch long and hairy. The twigs are slender and gray to brown in color. The fruits mature in July or August. They occur in small clusters and are covered by large conspicuous bracts. Each fruit is a nut that is ovoid to subglobose, light brown, and about ½ inch thick. These shrubs grow only in a few of Oklahoma's northeastern counties.

IRONWOOD

These trees are also known as Hop Hornbeam, Leverwood, and Deerwood. They are 20–30 feet tall and have rounded crowns with slender, drooping, often twisted branches. The leaves are simple, alternate, oval, pointed at their tips, uneven at the bases, and very sharply toothed. The blades are 3–5 inches long. These trees commonly occur as smaller understory trees and seem to prefer the dry, gravelly ridges of mountainous regions. The seeds are produced in distinctive, small, flattened nutlets that are enclosed in inflated saclike bracts which resemble those of the hop vine. These trees are restricted to the eastern half of Oklahoma.

CHINQUAPIN

These trees are also known as Chestnut Bush and Dwarf Chestnut. They are small trees that occasionally reach heights of 15–30 feet but are usually more shrublike. They occur in rich, moist soils of lowlands or slopes. The leaves are alternate, oblong-lanceolate, or narrowly oval with pointed tips. They are sharply serrate, 3–5 inches long, and have short petioles. The fruits are globose prickly burs that are 1–1½ inches in diameter and contain 2–3 ovoid nuts. These small trees occur at rare intervals in the eastern part of Oklahoma.

WHITE OAK
Quercus alba

Beech Family
Fagaceae

SWAMP WHITE OAK
Quercus bicolor

Beech Family
Fagaceae

22

NORTHERN RED OAK
Quercus borealis

Beech Family
Fagaceae

WHITE OAK

Other local names are Stave Oak, Fork-leaf White Oak, and Ridge White Oak. They are large trees, commonly reaching a height of 150 feet, with broad crowns. The leaves are alternate, simple, oblong or oval, and 5–9 inches long, with 7–11 rounded lobes. The twigs are slender, brownish to gray, and smooth. The fruiting acorns ripen in September or October and are ¾–1 inch long with cups encasing ¼ of their length. These trees are fairly common on the rich uplands and bottomlands of the eastern counties of Oklahoma.

SWAMP WHITE OAK

These trees are large and have domelike crowns. They often reach a height of 100 feet or more. The leaves are simple, alternate, 4–7 inches long, and 3–4 inches wide. Their margins are wavy-toothed or somewhat lobed. The petioles are ¼–¾ inch long, slender, and sturdy. The acorns are usually paired and are ovoid in form. They are borne in bowllike cups that cover more than half of the fruits. These trees are found in low, rich bottomland soils of Oklahoma's eastern counties.

NORTHERN RED OAK

These trees are also known locally as Leopard Oak, Gray Oak, Mountain Red Oak, Champion Oak, Black Oak, and Spanish Oak. They are large trees with rounded crowns and spreading branches. The twigs are reddish brown and lustrous. The leaves are alternate, simple, 5–9 inches long, 4–6 inches broad, and have 7–11 lobes. The acorns are single or paired, ovoid, pale brown when mature (October or November), and 2–4 times as long as their cups. These trees are widely distributed in the eastern third of Oklahoma, where they grow on slopes or bottomlands.

SOUTHERN RED OAK
Quercus falcata

Beech Family
Fagaceae

SWAMP CHERRYBARK OAK
Quercus falcata,
var. *pagodaefolia*

Beech Family
Fagaceae

SHINNERY OAK
Quercus Havardii

Beech Family
Fagaceae

SOUTHERN RED OAK

These trees are also known as Spanish Oak. They are freely branched and reach a height of 80 feet or more. The leaves are simple, alternate, extremely variable in form, and 6–7 inches long. The petioles are flattened, slender, and 1–2 inches long. The acorns are solitary or paired, globular or hemispheric, and about ½ inch long. They are enclosed at the bases in shallow cups and mature during the second season of growth. These trees grow in moist, rich soil or on gravelly mountain slopes of the southeastern counties of Oklahoma.

SWAMP CHERRYBARK OAK

These trees are also known as Swamp Red Oak, Swamp Spanish Oak, and Pagoda-leaf Oak. They may reach a height of more than 100 feet with a trunk diameter of 4–6 feet. The branches are large and form broad crowns. The bark is light gray with darker bands that resemble those of the black cherry. The leaves are alternate, simple, dark green above, 3–6 inches long, and have 5–11 pointed, up-turned tips. They are typically found in the low, poorly drained soils of the southeastern corner of Oklahoma. The acorns are borne singly or in pairs. They are about ½ inch long, rounded, and have shallow cups.

SHINNERY OAK

These low shrubs are also known as Sand Oak, Havard Shin Oak, Sand Scrub, and Panhandle Shinnery. They seldom reach a height of more than 4 feet and form thickets by means of underground rhizomes. The leaves are alternate, simple, and leathery and are 1–4 inches long. The leaf margins are usually coarsely toothed or lobed. The acorns are solitary or two to three in each cluster, and chestnut brown in color. These plants sometimes hybridize with Shin Oak (**Quercus mohriana**) or Post Oak (**Quercus stellata**). They are found in a few of Oklahoma's western counties where they grow in deep sand.

OVERCUP OAK
Quercus lyrata

Beech Family
Fagaceae

BUR OAK
Quercus macrocarpa

Beech Family
Fagaceae

BLACKJACK OAK
Quercus marilandica

Beech Family
Fagaceae

OVERCUP OAK

These trees are also known as Water White Oak, Swamp White Oak, Swamp Post Oak, and White Oak. They may attain a height of 100 feet and a trunk diameter of 2–3 feet. The leaves are alternate, simple, and 3–10 inches long and have several rounded lobes. The petioles are ⅓–1 inch long. The acorns are solitary or paired, ovoid, chestnut brown, ½–1 inch long, and almost covered by their cups. These trees grow in wet soils of far southeast Oklahoma.

BUR OAK

These trees are also known as Mossy Oak, White Oak, Scrub Oak, Blue Oak, and Overcup Oak. They are mostly large trees that reach a height of 60–150 feet, with trunks that are very large near the base and provide a broad, dome-like crown. They prefer rich, moist soil and are often found growing along streams. The leaves are very similar to those of the Post Oak, except that they reach a length of 4–6 inches and a breadth of 3–4 inches. The acorns are sessile with bowl-shaped cups. The nuts are ovoid, short, very broad, ½–⅔ inch long, and about ½ enclosed in the cups. The cups contain a distinctive fringe of fibers. They may be seen along streams and grow intermittently throughout all of Oklahoma except the Panhandle counties.

BLACKJACK OAK

These trees are also known as Jack Oak, Black Oak, Barren Oak, and Iron Oak. They are usually no more than 20–30 feet tall with a trunk width of one foot or less. The branches are strong, spreading, and slow-growing and form rounded crowns. They prefer barren, rocky slopes and are often associated with Post Oaks and Greenbriers. Their branches may die from the lower trunk upward and droop around the trees to provide an almost impenetrable base. These dead branches are very tough and durable, thus the name "Iron Oak." The leaves are broad, shallowly lobed, lustrous, simple, and alternately arranged. The acorns are about ¾ inch long, short-stalked, and their toplike cup covers half of the nut. These trees are widely distributed except in northwestern Oklahoma.

MOHR OAK
Quercus mohriana

Beech Family
Fagaceae

WATER OAK
Quercus nigra

Beech Family
Fagaceae

PIN OAK
Quercus palustris

Beech Family
Fagaceae

MOHR OAK

These small oaks are also known as Scrub Oak, Shin Oak, and Limestone Oak. They are usually thicket-forming shrubs but are occasionally round-topped trees that are 20 feet tall. The leaves are simple, alternate, oblong, and 1–4 inches long and have smooth or only slightly toothed margins. The fruiting acorns are solitary or in clusters of 2–3 and are 1/3–3/5 inch long. These plants grow in dry habitats of only a few of Oklahoma's northwestern counties.

WATER OAK

These trees are also known as Possum Oak and Swamp Oak. They reach a height of 50–80 feet and a trunk diameter of 2–4 feet. The crowns are broadly rounded. They typically inhabit low bottomlands, where they are very popular as shade trees for homes or meadow pastures. The leaves are simple, alternate, and quite variable in size and shape, even on the same tree. They are typically 2–4 inches long, 1–2 inches wide, and obovate with fairly even margins except near the apex, where there may be three small lobes. The acorns are almost black, short-ovate, and seated in shallow cups. They are about 1/2 inch long. These trees are limited to the eastern half of Oklahoma.

29

PIN OAK

These trees are also known as Swamp Spanish Oak, Swamp Oak, and Spanish Oak. They may reach a height of 100–120 feet. The lower branches usually droop toward their tips, providing an umbrellalike appearance. The leaves are simple, alternate, and 4–6 inches long with 5–9 lobes that are bristle-tipped. The acorns are solitary or clustered, sub-globose, about 1/2 inch thick, and light brown. The cups are shallow. These trees are very numerous in the northeastern counties and are often transplanted throughout Oklahoma. They thrive in the deep rich soils of lowlands.

WILLOW OAK
Quercus phellos

Beech Family
Fagaceae

**SCRUB CHESTNUT
OAK**
Quercus prinoides

Beech Family
Fagaceae

POST OAK
Quercus stellata

Beech Family
Fagaceae

WILLOW OAK

These trees are also known as Water Oak, Peach Oak, and Sandjack Oak. They commonly reach a height of more than 60 feet; on rare occasions they grow as high as 90 feet. They prefer low, poorly drained soils. The leaves are simple, alternate, and fairly distinctive among those of the other oaks. They are 2–4 inches long, $3/8$–$3/4$ inch broad, entire, and tipped with short bristles. The petioles are only $1/8$ inch long. The acorn fruits are almost globular, about $3/8$ inch long, and pale brown and are only $1/3$ enclosed in the cups. These trees are restricted to the eastern half of Oklahoma.

SCRUB CHESTNUT OAK

These trees are also known as Dwarf Chestnut Oak, Running White Oak, and Chinkapin Oak. They are small trees or shrubs that often are only 2–4 feet tall, but occasionally they reach heights of 12–15 feet. They grow on dry, rocky, or sandy soil along roadsides or on hillsides. The leaves are 3–5 inches long and 1–3 inches broad with short, sturdy petioles. They are simple, alternate, and oval and have coarsely serrate margins. The acorns are on short stalks with shallow pale cups. The nuts are less than an inch long and oval. They are about $2/3$ covered by the cups and light brown in color. These small trees or shrubs thrive in waste areas or pastures over a large area of Oklahoma.

POST OAK

These trees are also known as Turkey Oak, Box Oak, White Oak, and Iron Oak. They are small to medium-sized trees that seldom reach a height of 60 feet or a trunk diameter of more than one foot. They have dense, rounded crowns when the branches have an opportunity to grow freely. They typically grow in the poor, dry, rocky, or sandy soils of well-drained slopes. The leaves are alternate, simple, and 4–6 inches long and have about 5 rounded lobes. They are stiff, leathery, and slightly rough on the lower surfaces. The acorns are sessile with shallow cups. The nuts are ovoid, $1/2$–$2/3$ inch long, and about $1/3$ enclosed in the cups. Oklahoma represents the western limit of their range, but they may be found over almost all of the state.

RUDDY POST OAK
Quercus stellata,
var. *rufescens*

Beech Family
Fagaceae

WAVY-LEAF OAK
Quercus undulata

Beech Family
Fagaceae

BLACK OAK
Quercus velutina

Beech Family
Fagaceae

RUDDY POST OAK

These trees are considered by most researchers to be hybrids of Post Oak and Havard's Oak. This is very likely the correct interpretation. The trees are actually much smaller than the shrublike Havard's Oak. Other features, however, such as leaf forms, indicate a definite relationship with the above distinct species. They grow in the deep sands of hills and plains in the western counties of Oklahoma.

WAVY-LEAF OAK

These plants are also known as Scrub Oak, Shin Oak, and Switch Oak. The leaves are simple, alternate, coarsely toothed, oblong, and 1–2½ inches in length. The acorns grow in shallow cups and are about ½ inch long. They occur singly or paired. These small oaks grow in thickets and seem to thrive best on high, rocky slopes. In Oklahoma they occur only in the Black Mesa region of Cimarron County.

33

BLACK OAK

These trees are also known as Yellow-bark Oak. They are 80–90 feet tall and have spreading crowns. The leaves are simple, alternate, oval, and 4–10 inches long. They have 5–7 bristle-tipped lobes. The acorns are solitary or paired, ½–1 inch long, and ovoid to oblong in shape. They are borne in cups that are ¾–1 inch broad. These trees occupy dry, sandy, clayey, or gravelly soils throughout the eastern half of Oklahoma.

LIVE OAK
Quercus virginiana

Beech Family
Fagaceae

SUGARBERRY
Celtis occidentalis

Elm Family
Ulmaceae

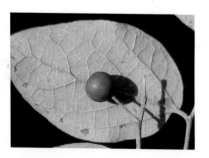

**WESTERN
HACKBERRY**
Celtis reticulata

Elm Family
Ulmaceae

LIVE OAK

These trees usually have massive trunks and wide-spreading branches, especially where they have deep, rich soil for maximum growth. When these conditions do not exist, the trees may be almost shrublike but still produce spreading branches. The leaves are alternate, simple, stiff, oblong-oval, entire, 2–5 inches long, and ½–2 inches wide. They are usually evergreen, at least in part, which adds to their value as ornamental plants. The fruits are acorns that are ¾–1 inch long, broadly oval, and about ½ enclosed in their cups. These trees are limited to southwest Oklahoma.

SUGARBERRY

These trees are also known as Nettle Tree, False Elm, Beaverwood, Hackberry, Juniper Tree, One-berry, and Rim Ash. They are relatively small trees that reach a height of 25–40 feet and have trunks that are 1–2 feet in diameter. The crown spreads and provides a rounded top. The bark of all hackberries or sugarberries is very rough with corky lumps that hang on for long periods. They prefer rich, moist soils but can survive, although in a much smaller form, on well-drained slopes. They are often seen around the bases of other kinds of trees, where they have grown from seeds dispersed by birds. The leaves are rough, simple, alternate, serrate-margined, ovate, sharply tipped, and 2–4 inches long. The fruits of this widely distributed tree are dark purple to brown and mature in September.

WESTERN HACKBERRY

These trees are also known as Sugarberry, Thick-leaved Hackberry, and Netleaf Hackberry. They rarely reach a height of more than 20 feet and have open crowns with stout branches. They grow on rocky hillsides and seem to prefer moderately dry soil. The leaves are not more than 3 inches long. They are alternately arranged, broadly ovate, and mostly lack teeth on their margins. They have conspicuous veins on the underneath surface. The fruits are ¼ inch long, almost globular, orange to yellow, and mature in October or September. The bark is rough and warty. They are abundant except in a few eastern counties.

WINGED ELM
Ulmus alata

Elm Family
Ulmaceae

AMERICAN ELM
Ulmus americana

Elm Family
Ulmaceae

CEDAR ELM
Ulmus crassifolia

Elm Family
Ulmaceae

WINGED ELM

These trees are also known as Cork Elm and Wahoo. They have prominent corky wings along the smaller branches. The branches form a rounded top, and they seldom grow to a height of more than 40 feet. They thrive best on well-drained soils and are very seldom seen in lowlands. The leaves are elliptical and nonsymmetrical at the base. They are 1–3 inches long, sharply pointed at the tips, simple, alternate, and doubly serrate on the margins. The petioles are very short. The fruits are produced before the leaves and are quickly dispersed. Each fruit is a flattened samara that is single-seeded and ¼ inch long. These trees are common along roadsides and among other trees in eastern Oklahoma.

AMERICAN ELM

These trees are also known as White Elm, Gray Elm, Water Elm, and Swamp Elm. The trunk typically divides rather low into two or more arching and ascending branches, which in turn branch and rebranch to form a broadly rounded and balanced crown. They often reach a height of 80–100 feet with a trunk diameter of 4–6 feet. They are among our most beautiful trees. They prefer the deep, rich soils of valleys or stream banks. The leaves are oval but have bases that are tapered to the tips. They are 3–5 inches long and have doubly serrate margins. The petioles are very short. The fruits are flat achenes that are ⅓–½ inch long with hairs only on their margins. They begin to appear before the emergence of leaves and are dispersed soon after the leaves are produced. These trees are distributed throughout all of Oklahoma except the Panhandle section.

CEDAR ELM

These trees branch less from the lower trunk than do most of our elms and are therefore tall and straight with high crowns. They reach heights of up to 70 feet with much interlacing of high branches. The leaves are alternate, simple, 1–2 inches long, narrowly ovate, slightly oblique basally, and doubly serrate. The petioles are very short. The fruits, hairy throughout, mature in early spring. These trees occur in southeast Oklahoma.

OSAGE ORANGE
Maclura pomifera

Mulberry Family
Moraceae

WHITE MULBERRY
Morus alba

Mulberry Family
Moraceae

38

BLACK MULBERRY
Morus nigra

Mulberry Family
Moraceae

OSAGE ORANGE

These trees are also known as Bowwood, Bois d'Arc, Hedge Apple, and Horse Apple. They are 20–30 feet tall with trunk diameters of about one foot. They have stiff, spiny, interlacing branches. They have been planted in various areas to serve as windbreaks or "living fences." They have sometimes become a greater nuisance than a help, however, because they shade adjoining fields and spread into other areas. The leaves are simple, alternate, and ovate with pointed tips and entire margins. The blades are 3–5 inches long and the petioles are 1–3 inches long. The fruits are composed of masses of packed drupes which collectively have the appearance of oranges. They are 3–5 inches in diameter and green when young, but they become yellow at maturity. These trees are well established east of Interstate 35 and south of Interstate 40 in Oklahoma.

WHITE MULBERRY

These trees are also known as Morea, Silkworm Mulberry, and Russian Mulberry. They grow to heights of as many as 40 feet and have broad, rounded crowns. The leaves are simple, alternate, glossy, lobed or unlobed, coarsely serrate, and 1–7 inches long. The fruits are white to pink, oval or oblong, and ½–¾ inch long. They mature in June, July, or August. These trees have escaped from cultivation and are now found along roadsides, in old fields, and in thickets. They are more numerous in Oklahoma's central and western counties.

BLACK MULBERRY

These small trees are also known as Hedge Mulberry and Glossy Mulberry. They have many spreading branches that grow from short trunks. The leaves are smooth, glossy, simple, alternate, oval, 2–6 inches long, and coarsely toothed on the margins. Occasionally they may be irregularly lobed. The mature fruits are dark red to black, fleshy, oblong, and ⅓–1 inch long. These trees have escaped from cultivation in many areas and may be found in roadside drains or in abandoned gardens and fields.

RED MULBERRY
Morus rubra

Mulberry Family
Moraceae

FOUR-WING SALTBUSH
Atriplex canescens

Goosefoot Family
Chenopodiaceae

COMMON PAWPAW
Asimina triloba

Custard-apple Family
Annonaceae

RED MULBERRY

These trees are 20–30 feet tall with trunk diameters of 1–1½ feet. The trunks are short and the branches are often irregular, forming broad, dense, rounded crowns. They occur scattered among other hardwood trees in rich, moist soils. The leaves are alternate, simple, cordate, serrate, and 3–5 inches long. They are quite often irregularly lobed. The flowers are small and inconspicuous in compact clusters. The fruits are oval, about an inch long, and sweet-tasting. They are black when they mature in July. These small trees are widely distributed in Oklahoma, occurring in all except a very few westernmost counties.

FOUR-WING SALTBUSH

These plants are also known as Wing Scale, Shad Scale, Sagebrush, Cenizo, Chamiso, Chamiza, and Costillas de Vaca. They are erect shrubs that are evergreen and 5–8 feet tall. The flowers are inconspicuous and borne on terminal twigs. The fruits mature in August or September, have two pairs of wings, and are ¼–½ inch long. These shrubs grow in grassy uplands, sandy deserts, or salt plains and are sparsely but widely distributed in the western half of Oklahoma.

COMMON PAWPAW

These shrubs or small trees are also known as Fetid Shrub and Custard Apple. They are most likely to develop as spreading shrubs with divergent lower branches but occasionally ascend to a height of 20–40 feet. The leaves are alternate, simple, oblong to obovate, and have entire margins. They are 4–12 inches long and have short, stout petioles. The flowers are purple to green and 1–2 inches broad. They appear with or before the leaves. The fruits are banana-like and 2–7 inches long. They are brown to black when mature. These plants are widely distributed in the low, moist valleys of the eastern one-fourth of Oklahoma.

**COMMON
SASSAFRAS**
Sassafras albidum

Laurel Family
Lauraceae

WILD HYDRANGEA
Hydrangea arborescens

Saxifrage Family
Saxifragaceae

**PRICKLY
GOOSEBERRY**
Ribes cynosbati

Saxifrage Family
Saxifragaceae

COMMON SASSAFRAS

Other local names are Ague Tree, Saloop, Gumbo Filé, Cinnamon Stick, and Smelling Stick. These trees are 40–90 feet tall and have flattened crowns. The leaves are simple, alternate, aromatic, ovate, and are either entire or divided into 2–3 mittenlike lobes. The petioles are about an inch long. The mature twigs are often reddish in color. The fruits are single-seeded drupes that are blue, lustrous, about ½ inch long, and oblong or globose. They are borne on red stalks. These trees are widely distributed in the eastern third of the state.

WILD HYDRANGEA

These shrubs are also known as Smooth Hydrangea, Sevenbark, Mountain Hydrangea, and Hill-of-Snow. They are scraggly, freely branched, 2–10 feet tall, and grow in clumps. The leaves are simple, opposite, broadly ovate, 2–6 inches long, and have serrate margins. The petioles are slender and 1–4 inches long. The flowers mature in June or July and occur in large clusters. The fruits mature in late autumn. Each one is a dry capsule that is 1/12–1/8 inch long. These plants grow only in a few of Oklahoma's northeastern counties, where they thrive along the ravines of upper slopes.

PRICKLY GOOSEBERRY

These shrubs are also known as Pasture Gooseberry, Dogberry, and Spiny Gooseberry. They grow in rocky woods or meadows and are 1–4 feet tall. The branches are pale brown or grayish and have slender spines at the nodes. The leaves are generally cordate (heartlike) in form but 5-lobed with serrate margins. The blades are soft and hairy on both sides and 1–2½ inches wide. The flowers are small and greenish. They grow in clusters of 2 or 3 and appear in April or June. The fruits are reddish purple, 1/3–½ inch in diameter, prickly, and ripen from July to September. These shrubs are restricted to the pinewoods of southeastern counties.

GOOSEBERRY
Ribes odoratum

Saxifrage Family
Saxifragaceae

COMMON WITCH HAZEL
Hamamelis virginiana

Witch Hazel Family
Hamamelidaceae

SWEET GUM
Liquidambar Styraciflua

Witch Hazel Family
Hamamelidaceae

GOOSEBERRY

These shrubs are also known as Golden Currant, Buffalo Currant, Missouri Currant, Clove Currant, and Flowering Currant. They are spreading or upright plants that have long, slender branches, mostly from near the bases. They ordinarily are no more than 6–8 feet tall. They prefer margins of streams or ravines where they become part of the undergrowth among the trees and vines. The leaves are simple, alternate, 1–3 inches long, and 3- to 5-lobed. The flowers are yellow, tubular, and very striking in appearance. The fruits are reddish to black when mature and 1/4–1/2 inch in diameter. They mature in August and are consumed by birds and small mammals. These small shrubs are widely distributed but do not seem to be thickly populated in dry regions.

COMMON WITCH HAZEL

These shrubs or small trees are also known as Witch Elm, Snappy Hazel, Pistachio, Tobacco Wood, Spotted Alder, and Winterbloom. The leaves are simple, alternate, oval, wavy-toothed, 1–6 inches long, and 1/2–3 inches broad. The flowers appear in October or November and are bright yellow. The fruits are woody capsules that develop during the following season. They are 1/2–1 inch long and ovoid in form. These shrubs grow in the rich, moist, sandy soils of ravines or stream margins. They are found in only a few of Oklahoma's eastern counties.

SWEET GUM

These trees are also known as Red Gum, Star-leaved Gum, Satin Walnut, Opossum Tree, Bilsted, White Gum, Alligator Tree, and Liquidambar. They are large trees, becoming 60–80 feet tall with trunk diameters of 2–4 feet. In open areas they branch very symmetrically to form broad crowns. They prefer swamps or moist lowlands. The leaves are simple, alternate, star-shaped, and usually 5-lobed. The blades are 4–7 inches long and the petioles are 3–5 inches long. The fruits of these southeastern Oklahoma trees are 2-beaked, globose capsules that become dry and spiny. They hang from long pedicels and often remain attached in the winter.

SYCAMORE
Platanus occidentalis

Plane-tree Family
Platanaceae

**DOWNY
SERVICEBERRY**
Amelanchier arborea

Rose Family
Rosaceae

46

**MOUNTAIN
MAHOGANY**
Cercocarpus montanus

Rose Family
Rosaceae

SYCAMORE

These trees are also known as Buttonball, Buttonwood, Plane Tree, and Water Beech. They are among the largest of our trees, occasionally reaching heights of 100–175 feet with trunk diameters of 3–8 feet. They branch rather extensively to form open crowns. They thrive best in low, moist, rich soils. The leaves are alternate, simple, broadly ovate, lobed, and coarsely toothed. They are often 4–8 inches long. The petioles are stout, 1–3 inches long, and enclose the axillary buds at their bases. The fruits are globular and are attached by long, weak peduncles. At maturity each fruit is dry, about an inch thick, yellow to brown, and contains many fiber-covered seeds. These trees are mostly found in eastern Oklahoma and are fairly numerous.

DOWNY SERVICEBERRY

These shrubs or small trees are also known as Shadbush, Shadlow, Boxwood, Billberry, June Plum, Indian Cherry, Swamp Shadbush, Indian Pear, Juice Pear, Sugar Pear, and Berry Pear. They grow along ravines and lower slopes of hillsides. The leaves are simple, alternate, oval, finely serrate, and 2–5 inches long. The flowers develop in March or April. They are borne 6–12 in a cluster and each has 5 white petals. The fruits mature in June or July. They are globose, reddish purple, and ¼–½ inch thick. Although these plants are often cultivated, they are widely distributed in natural habitats in the eastern half of Oklahoma.

MOUNTAIN MAHOGANY

These plants are also known as True Mountain Mahogany, to be distinguished from Silver Mountain Mahogany and Shaggy Mountain Mahogany, which are separate varieties of this species. They are shrubs or small trees that are 12 feet tall or less. The leaves are simple, alternate, and usually clustered on very short lateral branches. Each leaf is broadly oval to obovate and has a serrate margin. The fruits are ⅓–⅖ inch long with unique silky, featherlike tails that are 1–3 inches long. These plants are found only in the Black Mesa region of Oklahoma's Cimarron County.

THORN APPLE
Crataegus crus-galli

Rose Family
Rosaceae

48

PARSLEY HAW
Crataegus marshallii

Rose Family
Rosaceae

DOWNY HAW
Crataegus mollis

Rose Family
Rosaceae

THORN APPLE

These trees are also known as Cockspur Thorn, Red Haw, Pinthorn, and Hawthorn. They have spreading or ascending branches which form rounded or tapered crowns. The stems contain long spines which are very rigid and sharp-tipped. They prefer open woods or rocky slopes. The leaves are alternate, simple, oval, serrate, and 1–2 inches long. The petioles are short. The flowers are pinkish to almost white, about an inch in diameter, and very numerous. They appear in April, quickly following leaf enlargement. The fruits are globose, red, and about ½ inch thick. Although these trees are widely distributed, they are not found in great numbers in any section of Oklahoma.

PARSLEY HAW

These plants are also known as Parsley Hawthorn and Parsley-leaved Thorn. They are slender shrubs or small trees that are no more than 20 feet tall. The leaves are simple, alternate, ovate to orbicular, ¾–1½ inches long, and have 5–7 serrate lobes. The twigs are brown to gray, crooked, and have a few slender spines. The flowers have five white petals. The fruits are oblong or ovoid pomes that are bright red and about ⅓ inch long when mature. These plants grow in low, rich soils in a few of Oklahoma's southeastern counties.

DOWNY HAW

These trees are also known as Downy Thorn, Red Haw, Scarlet Haw, and Red-fruited Thorn. They are usually shrub-like, but occasionally they reach heights of 30–40 feet. They grow in a variety of habitats but are found most often in low prairies or meadows of pastures. The branches are profuse and contain a few spines that are 1–2 inches long. The leaves are alternate and simple with blades that are ovate to heart-shaped, 1–4 inches long, and toothed on the margins. The flowers are white to pink and about an inch broad. The fruits are globose, red with a few corky spots, and ½ inch in diameter. These fruits mature in September and may be retained after leaf fall. These trees are widely distributed in Oklahoma.

GREEN HAWTHORN
Crataegus viridis

Rose Family
Rosaceae

TRIFOLIATE ORANGE
Poncirus trifoliata

Rose Family
Rosaceae

CHICKASAW PLUM
Prunus angustifolia

Rose Family
Rosaceae

GREEN HAWTHORN

These small trees are also known as Green Thorn and Southern Thorn. They are seldom more than 25 feet tall and have a few thorns on the upper branches. The leaves are simple, alternate, serrate or doubly serrate, slightly lobed, and ¾–3 inches long. The flowers are about ¾ inch in diameter, white to pink, and borne in clusters. The fruits are globose pomes that may remain green but usually become red to orange when mature. These trees are found throughout the eastern half of Oklahoma.

TRIFOLIATE ORANGE

These little trees are sometimes known as Thornbush and Lemon Bush. Their branches, which are slender and somewhat drooping, spread from the lower trunks. These branches are unusually green in color and contain numerous stout spines. When the plants are used as hedges, they are pruned so that they become more compact in their growth. As a result of this use, they seem to be establishing themselves along streams in Oklahoma's southeastern counties, where I have encountered a few scattered trees. The leaves are compound with three leaflets. Each leaflet is 1–2 inches long, glossy, and slightly serrate. The fruits are lime-sized but lemonlike in color. These trees are very limited in distribution at this time but are known to be established in McCurtain County, Oklahoma.

CHICKASAW PLUM

These shrubby plants are sometimes known as Sand Plum, Red Plum, American Wild Plum, and Western Plum. They are freely branched and mostly 2–6 feet tall. Almost without exception they form thickets, and these occasionally may cover an acre of ground. They thrive best in sandy loam soils of prairies. The leaves are simple, alternate, serrate, oval, and 1–3 inches long. The flowers are pink to white and ½–1 inch in diameter. They appear slightly ahead of the leaves and add considerably to the beauty of the landscape in April. The fruits are globose, red or yellow, ½–1 inch thick, and quite edible. They mature in early fall. These shrubs are widely distributed.

TREE PLUM
Prunus mexicana

Rose Family
Rosaceae

BLACK CHERRY
Prunus serotina

Rose Family
Rosaceae

WESTERN CRAB APPLE
Pyrus ioensis

Rose Family
Rosaceae

TREE PLUM

These trees are also known as Mexican Plum and Mexican Cherry. They are slender trees that are 10–20 feet tall and do not form thickets as do most of our plums. They have slender, spreading branches that droop to form rounded crowns. The leaves are simple, oval, coarsely and irregularly serrate, and 1–3 inches long. The petioles are very short. The flowers are pink to white and about an inch in diameter. They appear slightly ahead of the leaves in early spring. At this time they are easy to spot along ravines or stream banks in woodlands. The fruits grow in small clusters from short lateral branches. Each one is yellow to reddish and about ¾ inch thick. These trees are widely distributed in Oklahoma.

BLACK CHERRY

These trees are also known as Cabinet Cherry, Whiskey Cherry, Wild Cherry, and Rum Cherry. They grow to heights of 50–60 feet with trunks that are 1–3 feet thick. The crowns are oblong and mostly irregular in outline. They grow best in deep, moist, fertile soils. The leaves are alternate, simple, oval to lanceolate, finely serrate, and 2–5 inches long. The petioles are ½–1 inch long. The flowers are in long, loose racemes and are white. The fruits are purplish to black, spherical, pea-sized, and mature in late summer. These trees are restricted to the eastern half of Oklahoma.

WESTERN CRAB APPLE

These trees are also known as Wild Apple and American Crab Apple. They are small trees that somewhat resemble apple trees or pear trees. The leaves are alternate, simple, blunt-tipped, serrate, and 1–2 inches long. The flowers are white to pink, about an inch broad, and appear in April or May. The fruits are ½–¾ inch in diameter and globular in form. They are reddish to purple with corky spots on the surface. These trees grow in open woods, old fields, along roadsides, or in ravines. They are mostly found in Oklahoma's eastern counties except when they have been transplanted as landscape trees farther west.

ARKANSAS ROSE
Rosa arkansana

Rose Family
Rosaceae

SWAMP ROSE
Rosa carolina

Rose Family
Rosaceae

MULTIFLORA ROSE
Rosa multiflora

Rose Family
Rosaceae

ARKANSAS ROSE

These plants are erect shrubs that are not more than 2 feet tall and have very bristly or prickly stems. The leaves are alternate and pinnately compound. The leaflets are 9–11 in number, elliptic, serrate, and ½–2½ inches long. The flowers appear in the summer months. They are white to pink and 1–3 inches broad. The fruits are pomes that are globose, red when mature, and ½–¾ inch thick. These small shrubs are found on rocky slopes or dry prairies and are widely distributed, although infrequent. They were first found on the banks of the Arkansas River of Colorado, which accounts for their name.

SWAMP ROSE

These shrubs are also known as Wild Rose and Hip Tree. They are commonly found in thickets along fences. They may be erect and 5–8 feet tall or, where support from fences or other structures is available, even taller. They may, by their own tangled growth, provide some of their own support. The stems are very thorny. The leaves are alternate, pinnately compound, and usually have seven leaflets. Each of the leaflets is mostly blunt and coarsely toothed. The fruits are globose and only about ¼ inch thick. They ripen in early fall and are retained during the winter. These plants grow in moist, open areas of Oklahoma's southeastern counties.

MULTIFLORA ROSE

These plants are small, freely branched shrubs that often climb over roadside fences or other shrubs. The leaves are alternate, pinnately compound, and have 5–9 leaflets. Each leaflet is 1–2 inches long, oval, and has a serrate margin. The flowers are white to pink, ½–1 inch broad, and have five petals. The fruits are red when mature. They are about ¼ inch thick and are globular or pear-shaped. These plants have escaped from cultivation and have become well established. They seem to be most abundant in the eastern half of Oklahoma.

WILD ROSE
Rosa setigera

Rose Family
Rosaceae

SOUTHERN BLACKBERRY
Rubus louisianus

Rose Family
Rosaceae

56

OZARK BLACKBERRY
Rubus ozarkensus

Rose Family
Rosaceae

WILD ROSE

These shrubs are also known as Prairie Rose, Climbing Rose, Michigan Rose, and Rose-blush. They grow in small thickets and are most often seen along roadside drains or small ravines. They branch from the stem bases and often are 5–10 feet tall. The leaves are alternate, pinnately compound, and have three or more leaflets. The leaflets are irregularly serrate or slightly lobed and 1–2 inches long. The flowers are pink to white and 2–3 inches in diameter. The fruits are globose, red, and usually about an inch thick. They mature in early autumn and may be retained all winter. These shrubby plants are widely distributed in the eastern and southern sections of Oklahoma.

SOUTHERN BLACKBERRY

These small shrubs are also known as Dewberry and Louisiana Blackberry. They are 1–5 feet tall, spreading to form thickets, and very thorny. They prefer low, moist waste places. The leaves are alternate and compound with three leaflets. The leaflets are oval to lanceolate, serrate, and 1–3 inches long. The flowers are white and ½–1 inch in diameter. The fruits are at first red and finally become jet-black when they mature in early summer. They are oval in form, ⅓–⅔ inch long, and quite tasty. These small shrubs are restricted to the southeastern one-fourth of Oklahoma.

OZARK BLACKBERRY

These erect shrubs are 3–6 feet tall and have fewer thorns than most blackberry plants. The leaves have 3–5 leaflets. Each leaflet is 2–3 inches long, ¾–2 inches wide, and has serrate margins. The flowers are white, ¼–½ inch broad, and appear in May, June, or July. The fruits mature from July to September. They are black when mature and not more than ½ inch long. These plants grow in low woodlands of a few of Oklahoma's northeastern counties.

WILD BLACKBERRY
Rubus trivialis

Rose Family
Rosaceae

MIMOSA
Albizia julibrissin

Legume Family
Leguminosae

58

LEADPLANT
Amorpha canescens

Legume Family
Leguminosae

WILD BLACKBERRY

These small shrubs are also known as Brambleberry and
Low Bush Blackberry. They prefer low, moist, rich soils of
open woods or meadows. They are freely branched and
some stems are prostrate. The stems are well fortified with
small spines. They mostly form large thickets. The leaves
are pinnately compound with three leaflets. The leaflets are
broadly lanceolate to ovate and are more round than sharp
at the tips. They are serrate and 1–3 inches long. The flowers
are white and 1–1½ inches in diameter. The fruits are black
when mature, ovoid, and often an inch long. They are quite
tasty and are a great favorite with those who gather wild
fruits. These shrubs are widely distributed but are most
plentiful in the eastern portion of Oklahoma.

MIMOSA

Other local names for these trees are Silk Tree and Acacia.
They attain heights of up to 40 feet and have widely spreading and drooping branches. They are often broader than
their height. The leaves are alternate, twice-pinnately compound, and 10–15 inches long. The small leaflets are ¼–½
inch long, oblong, and number 8–30 per section. The flowers
grow in clusters and appear from May to August. They have
long, pink stamens which provide a striking appearance.
The fruits are legume pods that are 5–8 inches long and
almost an inch wide. These trees are fairly well established
along roadsides of the southeast ¼ of Oklahoma. They were
originally imported from tropical Asia as ornamental trees.

LEADPLANT

These shrubs are also known as Wild Tea and Shoestrings.
They are usually only 1–3 feet tall and are branched from the
base but usually not branched above. Their choice habitat
seems to be prairies and slopes, they grow in a variety of soil
types. The leaves are alternate, pinnately compound, white-
hairy, rather compact, and 2–4 inches long. They have 21–
51 leaflets which are ¼–½ inch long and oblong or oval.
The flowers are in long spikes; each is bright blue to pinkish
and about ¹⁄₁₆ inch long. The fruits of this widely distributed
shrub are legume pods that are 1-seeded and very small.

BLACK DALEA
Dalea frutescens

Legume Family
Leguminosae

HONEY LOCUST
Gleditsia triacanthos

Legume Family
Leguminosae

COFFEE TREE
Gymnocladus dioicus

Legume Family
Leguminosae

BLACK DALEA

These shrubs are also known as Western Dalea. They branch from the base and have very slender, wiry twigs that are green to reddish brown. They are usually 1–3 feet tall. The leaves are alternate and pinnately compound with 13–17 leaflets. Each leaflet is ¼–½ inch long and about ⅛–¼ inch wide. The flowers are purple, very small, and borne in short, compact spikes. The fruits contain one or two seeds and are flattened pods. These small shrubs grow on well-drained, rocky slopes. They seem to be restricted to the Arbuckle Mountain area of Oklahoma.

HONEY LOCUST

These trees are also known as Sweet Locust, Black Locust, Thorn Locust, and Three-thorned Locust. The trunks are usually short and divided into several branches. These continue to branch, forming broadly rounded crowns. They grow naturally in rich bottomlands where limestone soils exist. They adapt fairly well to different habitats, where they thrive in thickets. The leaves are alternate, pinnately or twice-pennately compound, and contain from few to many ultimate segments. Each leaf segment is ½–1½ inches long, oblong-lanceolate, and finely serrate. The twigs contain spines that are frequently branched. The fruits are legume pods that are 10–18 inches long, slightly twisted, and dark brown or black when mature. These trees are widely distributed in the eastern half of Oklahoma.

63

COFFEE TREE

These trees are also known as Coffee Bean, Lucky Bean, Coffey Nut, Stump Tree, Kentucky Coffee Tree, Kentucky Mahogany, and Chicot. They attain a height of 80–100 feet. The leaves are alternate and twice-compound. The leaflets are 1–3 inches long, oval, and sharply pointed. The flowers appear in May or June and are greenish white. The fruits mature in late summer. They are flat, thick, broad, green to brown, 4–10 inches long, and contain several seeds. The seeds are dark brown and very hard. These trees grow in moist rich soils and are widely distributed but not numerous.

CATCLAW
Mimosa borealis

Legume Family
Leguminosae

MESQUITE
Prosopis glandulosa

Legume Family
Leguminosae

COMMON LOCUST
Robinia Pseudo-Acacia

Legume Family
Leguminosae

CATCLAW

These shrubs are also known as Thorny Mimosa and Cat-claw Mimosa. They are 5–10 feet tall with much branching and have hooked spines at the stem nodes. They prefer dry slopes that are gravelly or rocky. The leaves are alternate and pinnately twice-compound. The leaflets are oval, entire, and ⅙–⅓ inch long. The flowers are in compact hemispherical or global clusters that are ½–1 inch broad. Each flower has long, pink stamens which provide balllike masses of pink. These little shrubs are restricted in Oklahoma to several western counties.

MESQUITE

These trees are also known as Screw Bean. They are profusely branched, often from near the ground, and are 8–20 feet tall. Their crowns are broad and flattened or slightly rounded. Their twigs often possess small spines. The leaves are alternate and twice-pinnately compound. Each ultimate leaf segment is ½–2 inches long, quite narrow, and entire. The fruits are several-seeded legume pods that are 4–9 inches long, ¼–½ inch wide, and somewhat flattened. These small trees thrive in the entire western half of Oklahoma, but they are most plentiful in the southwest one-fourth, where they seem to prefer dry prairie pastures.

COMMON LOCUST

These trees are also known as Black Locust, Yellow Locust, White Locust, and Acacia. They are generally 30–70 feet tall with trunk diameters of 1–2½ feet. The crowns are irregularly oblong and rather open. Sprouts from the roots often form thickets. They grow best in deep, rich, moist bottomlands but are commonly found on drier limestone hills. The leaves are alternate and pinnately compound with 12–20 leaflets. There are no terminal leaflets. Each leaflet is oblong-ovate and 1–2 inches long. The flowers are white, ½–1 inch long, and borne in loose, drooping racemes. The fruit pods are smooth, about 2–4 inches long, and ½ inch broad. These trees are distributed over at least half of the state and are most common in southeastern Oklahoma.

CORAL BEAN
Sophora affinis

Legume Family
Leguminosae

WAFER ASH
Ptelea trifoliata

Rue Family
Rutaceae

PRICKLY ASH
*Xanthoxylum
Clava-Herculis*

Rue Family
Rutaceae

CORAL BEAN

These trees are also known as Pinch Pod. They reach heights of 18–20 feet with trunk thicknesses of 8–10 inches. The upper branches form rounded crowns. The bark of the trunks is dark reddish brown in color. The leaves are alternate and pinnately compound with 13–19 leaflets. The leaflets are oval to elliptic, 1–2 inches long, and have smooth margins. The flowers are cream-colored and almost an inch long. The fruits are legume pods that are 1–3 inches long, grayish black, and contain 1–8 seeds. They have noticeable constrictions between the seeds. These trees are good indicators of limestone soils. They usually grow on rocky slopes or on borders of prairie streams and ravines. They are most frequent in the Arbuckle Mountain region of Oklahoma.

WAFER ASH

These trees are also known as Hop Tree, Shrubby Trefoil, Ague Bark, Quinine Tree, Pickaway Anise, and Prairie Shrub. They are small trees that grow to heights of 15–20 feet with trunk diameters of 6–12 inches. They seem to prefer rocky or sandy slopes. The leaves are alternate and are divided into three leaflets. These leaflets are ovate, slightly serrate, 2–5 inches long, and 1–3 inches wide. The petioles are 2–4 inches long. The fruits are disklike, 2-seeded samaras that have yellowish veins on the wings. They are $\frac{1}{4}$–1 inch in diameter, borne in clusters, and persist on the stems through the winter. These trees are widely distributed.

PRICKLY ASH

These trees are also known as Sea Ash, Southern Prickly Ash, and Pepperwood. They are small, slender, freely branched, and prickly. They occasionally grow to a height of 15 feet with a trunk diameter of 6 inches. The leaves are alternate and pinnately compound with 5–19 leaflets which are stiff and glossy. The fruits are about $\frac{1}{6}$ inch long and oval in form. They mature in June. In the fall they open to release a single, glossy, black seed. They seem to prefer low, moist bottoms or stream banks and often form a part of the underbrush in dense or open woods. These little trees are only found in the southern half of Oklahoma.

TREE-OF-HEAVEN
Ailanthus altissima

Quassia Family
Simarubiaceae

CHINABERRY
Melia azedarach

Chinaberry Family
Meliaceae

SKUNKBUSH
Rhus aromatica

Sumac Family
Anacardiaceae

TREE-OF-HEAVEN

These trees are also known as Ailanthus (from their generic name), Chinese Sumac, Heavenward, False Varnish, and Devil's-Walking-Stick. They may reach heights of 40–90 feet. The leaves are pinnately compound and 1–3 feet long. The leaflets are 13–41 in number, lanceolate in form, and 2–6 inches long. The flowers are white to greenish, about ¼ inch broad, and grow in loose panicles. The fruits are small, twisted samaras. These trees have escaped from cultivation and become established along our roadsides, especially in sandy loam soil.

CHINABERRY

These trees are also known as China Tree, Pride-of-India, and Pride-of-China. They prefer the coastal plains of the southeastern United States and have been introduced into Oklahoma, where they have recently become naturalized. They are small trees with low, flattened crowns. The leaves are alternate and twice-pinnately divided into a large number of leaflets. Each leaflet is oval, tapered to a long tip, 1–2 inches long, and toothed on the margins. The fruits are globular, yellow drupes that are about ½ inch thick and borne in long, hanging clusters. In early summer they have large clusters of lilac-colored flowers. Although these small trees are widely distributed, they are not found in abundance in any specific part of Oklahoma.

SKUNKBUSH

These shrubs are also known as Fragrant Sumac and Sweet-scented Sumac. They are freely branched and only 3–8 feet tall. They form thickets in most instances. The leaves are alternate and pinnately compound and contain three leaflets. The leaflets are ovate, pointed at the tips, irregularly lobed on the margins, and 1–2 inches long. The flowers appear in April or May, before the leaves, and are yellow. The fruits are small, globose, and reddish yellow and are covered with short glandular hairs. The entire plant is aromatic with a faint skunklike odor, which is especially noticeable when a shoot is broken apart. These little shrubs are widely distributed in open, rocky woodlands.

WINGED SUMAC
Rhus copallina

Sumac Family
Anacardiaceae

SMOOTH SUMAC
Rhus glabra

Sumac Family
Anacardiaceae

POISON IVY
Rhus radicans

Sumac Family
Anacardiaceae

WINGED SUMAC

These are small trees or shrubs that are also known as Dwarf Sumac, Shining Sumac, Mountain Sumac, Upland Sumac, and Common Sumac. They seldom attain a height of more than 10 feet, though occasionally they may reach 15 feet. They grow most commonly on well-drained slopes and rocky ridges. The leaves are alternate, pinnately compound, and have 9–21 leaflets. The latter are lancelike, almost entire, and 1–3 inches long. The flowers are very small. The fruits are red and numerous, growing in terminal panicles. They are covered with short hairs that are also red. The fruits are each about ⅛ inch thick, globular, and very conspicuous because of their color and abundance.

SMOOTH SUMAC

These small trees or shrubs are also known as Upland Sumac, Scarlet Sumac, Sleek Sumac, Shoe-make, Senhal-anac, and Vinegar-tree. They seldom reach a height of more than 10 feet, with limited branching and smooth stems. They grow in thickets in old fields, open woods, or prairie pastures. The leaves are alternate and pinnately compound with 11–31 leaflets. Each leaflet is 2–4 inches long, lanceolate, serrate, and pointed at the tip. The flowers are greenish and inconspicuous. The fruits are red drupes about ⅙ inch in diameter and are covered with acid hairs. They are borne in large panicles. These sumacs are widely distributed.

71

POISON IVY

Other names for these plants are Poison Oak and Poison Rhus. They often grow as shrubs but may also be erect (and 1–3 feet tall), or prostrate. Perhaps most commonly they climb on adjacent trees, and when this occurs they may reach heights of 40–50 feet. The leaves are alternate and divided, forming 3 leaflets; they are attached by long petioles. The flowers are small and grow in loose racemes. The fruits are small, globular, white to light tan, and smooth. They mature in September. These plants are much feared, but many persons are not susceptible to the skin rash they can cause. They are widely distributed and difficult to avoid.

WINTERBERRY
Ilex decidua

Holly Family
Aquifoliaceae

AMERICAN HOLLY
Ilex opaca

Holly Family
Aquifoliaceae

YAUPON HOLLY
Ilex vomitoria

Holly Family
Aquifoliaceae

WINTERBERRY

These trees are also known as Swamp Holly, Deciduous Holly, Bearberry, and Possum Haw. They are small trees or shrubs that may be as tall as 25 feet. They occur along streams, on the borders of swamps, or on the slopes where moist soil exists. Unlike our other species of holly, the Winterberry loses all of its leaves in the fall. The leaves are 2–3 inches long and about ½–1 inch wide. They are narrowly oval, slightly toothed, alternate, simple, and have short petioles. The bright red fruits are about ⅓ inch in diameter. These trees are only found in eastern Oklahoma.

AMERICAN HOLLY

These trees are also known as Christmas Holly and White Holly. They are mostly small trees that reach heights of 15–20 feet, but some have been found that are as many as 40 feet tall. In Oklahoma most of these trees grow on gravelly slopes and are of the smaller variety. Some of them are male trees and lack the fruits that are found on the female trees. The leaves are alternate, simple, obovate in form, 2–4 inches long, and remain green and attached through the winter. They contain spine-tipped lobes, mostly toward the apices. The fruits are red, globular, and ⅓–½ inch in diameter. They mature in late fall. These trees occur in Oklahoma's southeastern counties where they are scattered over open woodlands, hillsides, and some lowlands.

YAUPON HOLLY

These trees are also known as Christmas Berry, Cassena, Emetic Holly, Appalachian Tea, Carolina Tea, and Indian Tea. They are shrubby trees that are slender and reach heights of 20 feet or less. They often form small, dense thickets. These plants are cultivated both for their beauty and for the tea that can be prepared from the leaves, which are alternate, simple, long-oval, and slightly toothed on the margins. They are 2–3 inches long and are retained for a time in the fall. The petioles are very short. The red fruits are ⅙–¼ inch thick and are retained even longer than the leaves. They are most frequent in the low, rich soils of eastern counties.

BURNING BUSH
Euonymus americana

Staff-tree Family
Celastraceae

EASTERN WAHOO
Euonymus
atropurpureus

Staff-tree Family
Celastraceae

74

BOX ELDER
Acer negundo

Maple Family
Aceraceae

BURNING BUSH

These are shrubs that are also known as Fishwood, Straw-berry Bush, and Bursting Heart. They are small, freely branched shrubs that are 2–8 feet tall. They sometimes form small thickets in low, moist woods or along streams. The leaves are opposite, simple, and 1–2 inches long. They are oval in form, pointed at the tips, and finely serrate. The flowers are greenish, disklike, and ½–1 inch broad. The fruits are capsules with wartlike external surfaces that may become pinkish to red before opening, when they expose red arils (the fleshy coverings of seeds). These little shrubs thrive in a few of Oklahoma's southeastern counties where they become most noticeable in October when the capsules open.

EASTERN WAHOO

These plants are also known as Spindle Tree, Bursting Heart, Bleeding Heart, Arrowwood, Indian Arrow, Bitter Oak, and Strawberry Tree. They are shrubs or small spindly trees that seldom exceed 25 feet in height. The leaves are opposite, simple, ovate, 2–5 inches long, and serrate. The flowers appear in May or June. They are purple, about ½ inch wide, and are grouped in small, loose clusters. The fruits are lobed and are about ½ inch broad when they mature in September or October. These plants grow along streams and are widely distributed.

BOX ELDER

These trees are also known as Ash-leaved Maple and Three-leaved Maple. They are small trees that occasionally become 50 feet tall. The trunk commonly divides into several spread-ing branches to form a rather open, irregular crown. They thrive on the banks of bottomland streams or swamps. The leaves are opposite and pinnately compound. The leaflets are usually 3 or 5 in number, 2–4 inches long, 1–3 inches broad, and ovate in outline. They have coarsely toothed margins and pointed tips. The petioles are 2–3 inches long. The fruits are typical maplelike samaras with large incurved wings and simple seeds. They are borne in drooping clusters, maturing in late summer. These trees are widely distributed.

RED MAPLE
Acer rubrum

Maple Family
Aceraceae

SILVER MAPLE
Acer saccharinum

Maple Family
Aceraceae

SUGAR MAPLE
Acer saccharum

Maple Family
Aceraceae

RED MAPLE

These trees are also known as Swamp Maple, Soft Maple, Water Maple, and White Maple. They have broad crowns and may reach a height of as many as 100 feet. The leaves are simple, opposite, coarsely serrate, and have 3–5 lobes. They are light green above and whitish below, turning yellowish orange or red in the fall. The fruits are paired samara that are 1–1½ inches long and mature in March or April. These trees are mostly restricted to lowlands in the eastern half of Oklahoma.

SILVER MAPLE

These trees are also known as Soft Maple, River Maple, Silverleaf Maple, White Maple, Creek Maple, Water Maple, and Swamp Maple. They are highly branched and 60–80 feet tall with broad crowns and trunk diameters of 2–4 feet. They are typically found on stream banks or in low, moist bottoms but will adapt to city landscapes. The leaves are opposite and simple and have blades that are 3–6 inches long, 3–6 inches broad, and deeply lobed with sharply tipped points on the lobes. The fruits are winged samara with the wings extending to lengths of 1–3 inches. They are borne in small clusters and mature in May, when they are soon dispersed by the wind. These trees are most plentiful in Oklahoma's northeastern counties but occasionally grow farther south and southwest.

SUGAR MAPLE

These trees are also known as Sweet Maple, Hard Maple, and Black Maple. They are often 100 feet tall and have broad, round-topped crowns. They thrive on low slopes. The leaves are simple, opposite, 3–6 inches long, and 3–6 inches wide. They usually contain 3–5 lobes that are slightly and irregularly toothed. They change from green to beautiful shades of yellow, orange, or red in autumn. The twigs are slender, glossy, and brown when mature. The fruits mature in September or October. They are samara that are red to brown and 1–1½ inches long. These trees are found only in the extreme eastern portion of Oklahoma.

OHIO BUCKEYE
Aesculus glabra

Horse-chestnut Family
Hippocastanaceae

RED BUCKEYE
Aesculus Pavia

Horse-chestnut Family
Hippocastanaceae

SOAPBERRY
Sapindus Drummondii

Soapberry Family
Sapindaceae

OHIO BUCKEYE

These trees or shrubs are also known as Fetid Buckeye, Stinking Buckeye, Horse Chestnut, and Lucky Bean. They are seldom taller than 20 feet in our region of the country. They branch very freely and have rounded crowns. The leaves are opposite, have long petioles, and are palmately compound with 5–9 leaflets. The leaflets are narrowly oval, finely serrate, and 3–4 inches long. The flowers are yellow and about ½–1 inch long. The fruits are yellow, spiny, and have 1–3 seeds, depending on the number that actually matures. These trees are widely distributed in Oklahoma and seem to prefer rich, moist, sandy slopes or valleys.

RED BUCKEYE

These are small shrubs which are usually 5–10 feet tall, but on rare occasions they may reach heights of 30 feet or more. The leaves are opposite, palmately compound, and usually have five leaflets. Each leaflet is oval, sharply serrate, and 4–8 inches long. The petioles are stout and 4–6 inches long. The flowers are fiery red, irregular in form, and 1–1½ inches long. The fruits are smooth, globular capsules, 1–2 inches in diameter, and contain 1–3 chestnut brown seeds. These shrubs grow in a few of Oklahoma's southeastern counties, where they seem to thrive in low meadows or open woods.

SOAPBERRY

These trees are also known as Indian Soap Tree, Drummond's Soapberry and China Tree. They are freely branched and are 40–50 feet tall with rounded crowns. They thrive best at the base of slopes or along stream banks in various soil types. The leaves are alternate and pinnately compound with 7–19 leaflets. Each leaflet is lanceolate, entire, and 2–4 inches long. The flowers are white, about ⅕ inch broad, and borne in loose clusters. The fruits are globose or oval, ½ inch thick, and are usually 1-seeded. They become brownish yellow when they mature, which is in October or November. These trees are distributed throughout our state.

SNOWBALL
Ceanothus americanus

Buckthorn Family
Rhamnaceae

LOTE BUSH
Condalia obtusifolia

Buckthorn Family
Rhamnaceae

CAROLINA BUCKTHORN
Rhamnus caroliniana

Buckthorn Family
Rhamnaceae

SNOWBALL

These little shrubs are also known as Redroot and Smaller Redroot. They are highly branched and 1–2 feet tall. The leaves are opposite with very short petioles. The blades are simple, broadly oval, serrate, and ½–1½ inches long. The flowers are white and borne in compact umbels that form oval clusters. They emerge slightly ahead of the leaves. These little shrubs thrive in gravelly or rocky soils of well-drained slopes. They seem to prefer limestone outcrops that are exposed, such as those of the Arbuckle Mountains, but are widely distributed.

LOTE BUSH

These are shrubs that are also known as Prairie Bush and Thornbush. They grow on arid slopes and are 3–5 feet tall. They branch from the base and often form ovoid or spherical growths that are five feet in diameter. The leaves are small, simple, alternate, and oblong to elliptic with entire margins and blunt tips. The flowers are small, whitish, and borne in clusters or short racemes. The fruits are gray to black and about ⅓ inch in diameter when they mature in July or August. These shrubs are found only in a few of Oklahoma's southwestern counties.

CAROLINA BUCKTHORN

These trees are also known as Indian Cherry and Yellow Buckthorn. They are small trees, seldom reaching a height of 30 feet. They occur most commonly along streams but are occasionally seen on hillsides. The leaves are simple, alternate, narrowly oval, and finely serrate. They are 2–6 inches long. The petioles are ½–1 inch long. The fruits are globular drupes that are black when mature, sweet-tasting, about ⅓ inch thick, and contain three nutlets. These small trees are restricted to the eastern half of Oklahoma.

CAROLINA LINDEN
Tilia caroliniana

Linden Family
Tiliaceae

SAINT-ANDREW'S-CROSS
Ascyrum hypericoides

Saint-John's-wort
Family
Hypericaceae

SHRUBBY SAINT-JOHN'S-WORT
Hypericum prolificum

Saint-John's-wort
Family
Hypericaceae

CAROLINA LINDEN

These trees are also known as Basswood, Lime Tree, White-wood, and Bee Basswood. They are large trees with irregular, rounded crowns. The leaves are simple, alternate, ovate or cordate, serrate, 5–6 inches long, and 3–4 inches wide. The petioles are 1–2 inches long. The fruits are dry, drupaceous, ¼–⅓ inch thick, ovoid or globose, and brown in color. These trees are found in rich, moist soils of several eastern Oklahoma counties.

SAINT-ANDREW'S-CROSS

These small shrubs are branched from the base, spreading or ascending to a height of 5–10 inches. The stems are somewhat flattened. The leaves are oblong-oval, sessile, entire, and ½–1½ inches long. The flowers are terminal and axillary. Each flower is enclosed or nearly enclosed by two large bracts. The petals are bright yellow. The fruits are capsules which are ovoid and about ⅙ inch long. These tiny shrubs are fairly numerous in dry soils of the eastern half of Oklahoma.

SHRUBBY SAINT-JOHN'S-WORT

These small shrubs are also known as Rock Rose, Paint Brush, and Broom Brush. They are branched from the base and 1–3 feet tall. The stems are occasionally 1 inch thick near the base. The leaves are very numerous with quite a diversity of size. They are narrowly oblong, tapered at the base, and ½–3 inches long. The flowers are borne in loose, spreading clusters. Each flower is ½–¾ inch broad and brownish yellow with many stamens. The fruits are 3-celled capsules that are ⅓–½ inch long. These little shrubs are widely distributed in the eastern section of Oklahoma.

SALT CEDAR
Tamarix gallica

Salt-cedar Family
Tamaricaceae

WESTERN PRICKLY PEAR
Opuntia compressa

Cactus Family
Cactaceae

WALKING-STICK CHOLLA
Opuntia imbricata

Cactus Family
Cactaceae

SALT CEDAR

These small trees are also known as Tamarisk and Pink Cedar. They grow in open areas and seem to thrive in old oil fields and along rivers, especially where the saline content of the soil is high. They are mostly shrublike in these habitats and readily form thickets. They have alternate, scalelike, feathery leaves that actually resemble conifers. The flowers are produced in terminal, compact panicles, and are light pink in color. The fruits are very small 3-valved capsules that contain many minute seeds. These little trees are now widely distributed throughout Oklahoma.

WESTERN PRICKLY PEAR

These plants are mostly prostrate and often form mats that are 10 feet or more in diameter. The stems are composed of flattened fleshy joints that are elliptic or ovate in form. They are pale green and 3–5 inches long. The spines are always solitary, ¾–1 inch long, and quite rigid. The flowers are yellow and 2–4 inches broad. The fruits are red, when mature, club-shaped, smooth, fleshy, and 1–2 inches long. They grow in dry, sandy, or rocky soils and are found mostly in western Oklahoma.

WALKING-STICK CHOLLA

These plants are also known as Tree Cactus, Cane Cactus, Velas de Coyote, Candelabrum Cactus, Devil's Rope, Coyote Prickly Pear, Cardenche, and Tuna Juell. They are shrubby plants that may reach a height of 8–9 feet. They occasionally form thickets. The flowers are 2–3 inches broad and purple. The fruits are yellow, dry when mature, 1–1½ inches long, and covered by long tubercles. They are quite numerous on the rocky slopes of Oklahoma's Cimarron County.

PENCIL CACTUS
Opuntia leptocaulis

Cactus Family
Cactaceae

PRICKLY PEAR
Opuntia tortispina

Cactus Family
Cactaceae

BLACK GUM
Nyssa sylvatica

Nyssa Family
Nyssaceae

PENCIL CACTUS

These plants are also known as Tasajillo. They are shrubs with cylindrical stems that reach a height of 3–5 feet. They have relatively few spines but are armed with numerous hooked bristles. The fruits are fleshy, red, pear-shaped, ½–¾ inch long, and contain many small seeds. They mature in August and remain attached during the following winter. These plants are found in a few of Oklahoma's southwestern counties where they grow in gravelly, well-drained soils.

PRICKLY PEAR

These shrubs are also known as Eastern Prickly Pear. They are mostly prostrate and mat-forming. The stems are composed of flattened, thick, fleshy joints that are ovate to elliptic in form, pale green, and 2–4 inches long. The spines are solitary or in small clusters, about an inch long, and very rigid. The fruits mature in September or October. They are obovate, 1–2 inches long, pink to red, fleshy, and many-seeded. These shrubs grow on well-drained rocky or gravelly slopes and are widely distributed.

BLACK GUM

These trees are also known as Black Tupelo, Pepperidge, Sour Gum, Bee Gum, Hornpine, Hornbine, Hornpipe, Hornbeam, Snag Tree, and Yellow Gum. They may reach a height of 100 feet. The leaves are simple, alternate, 2–6 inches long, and smooth-margined. The petioles are about one inch long. The fruits ripen in September or October and there are 1–3 in each cluster. They are blue to black in color, ovoid, and about ½ inch long. These trees are widely distributed in the eastern half of Oklahoma.

DEVIL'S-WALKING-STICK
Aralia spinosa

Ginseng Family
Araliaceae

ROUGH-LEAVED DOGWOOD
Cornus Drummondii

Dogwood Family
Cornaceae

FLOWERING DOGWOOD
Cornus florida

Dogwood Family
Cornaceae

DEVIL'S-WALKING-STICK

These trees are also known as Hercules'-Club, Angelica Tree, Prickly Ash, Prickly Elder, Pigeon Tree, and Toothache Tree. They are small spiny trees or shrubs that are slender and flat-topped. The leaves are very large, twice-pinnately compound, 3–4 feet long, and 2–4 feet broad. The individual leaflets are ovate, serrate, and 1–4 inches long. Their petioles are 18–20 inches long and encircle the stem at their bases. The flowers are in terminal panicles. They appear in July and are small but conspicuous because of their large numbers. The fruits are about ¼ inch in diameter, spherical, and black. I have seen these small trees growing on their own only in rich, moist soils along the woodland streams of McCurtain County.

ROUGH-LEAVED DOGWOOD

These shrubs are also known as Rough-leaved Cornel and Drummond's Dogwood. They are 3–15 feet tall and sparsely branched. They often grow in thickets and form a part of the underbrush of low woodlands. The leaves are simple oppo-site, thin, oval, and sharp-tipped. The flowers are numerous, white, and borne in loose terminal clusters. The fruits are off-white when mature, and ¼ inch in diameter. These widely distributed shrubs are common in south-central Oklahoma.

FLOWERING DOGWOOD

These trees are also known as Boxwood, White Cornel, Cornelian Tree, Nature's Mistake, and Indian Arrowwood. They are 13–30 feet tall with trunks that are 6–12 inches thick. The branches spread to form flat-topped crowns. They thrive on well-drained soils and often form an understory in oak-hickory forests. They also occur in old fields, fence rows, and roadsides. The leaves are opposite, simple, 3–5 inches long, and 2–3 inches wide. They are papery thin, point-tipped, and entire. The petioles are ½–¾ inch long. The flowers are in compact clusters surrounded by four large, white-to-pink bracts that are very striking. The ½-inch fruits mature in September. These small trees are restricted to eastern Oklahoma.

PRIVET ANDROMEDA
Lyonia ligustrina

Heath Family
Ericaceae

SPARKLEBERRY
Vaccinium   arboreum

Heath Family
Ericaceae

DEERBERRY
Vaccinium stamineum

Heath Family
Ericaceae

PRIVET ANDROMEDA

These shrubs are also known as Whitewood, White Alder, Pepperbush, Seedy Buckberry, Lyon's Andromeda, and He-huckleberry. They are highly branched and 3–12 feet tall. The leaves are alternate, firm, elliptic, and 1–3 inches long. The fruits are dry when mature, globular, ⅛–⅙ inch long, and have five sutures that are riblike. These plants are found in sandy soild of woodland slopes, especially where plenty of moisture is available. They are mostly seen in Oklahoma's southeastern counties.

SPARKLEBERRY

These shrubs or small trees are also known as Tree Huckleberry and Farkleberry. They are 4–30 feet tall and irregularly branched, often forming an umbrellalike appearance. The leaves are glossy, firm, obovate, ½–2 inches long, and have very short petioles. The flowers are few in short racemes. They are white, almost globular, and about ⅕ inch long. The fruits are black, globular, about ¼ inch thick, and mature in July or August. These small plants are widely distributed in sandy or rocky woodlands of most of the eastern counties of Oklahoma.

DEERBERRY

These plants are also known as Squaw Huckleberry and Buckberry. They are irregularly branched shrubs and are no more than 6 feet tall. The leaves are simple, alternate, oblong to oval, entire-margined, and ½–3 inches long. The smallest leaves are on the floral branches. The flowers mature in April, May, or June. They are white, ¼–⅓ inch broad, and are often solitary in the leaf axes. The fruits mature in September. They are globose and green or yellowish. These small shrubs grow in moist, sandy, acid soils of a few of Oklahoma's easternmost counties.

BLUE HUCKLEBERRY
Vaccinium vacillans

Heath Family
Ericaceae

**RABBITEYE
BLUEBERRY**
Vaccinium virgatum

Heath Family
Ericaceae

CHITTAMWOOD
Bumelia lanuginosa

Sapodilla Family
Sapotaceae

BLUE HUCKLEBERRY

These shrubs are also known as Low Huckleberry and Early Sweet Blueberry. They are ½–3 feet tall and highly branched. The leaves are simple, alternate, elliptic to oval, ¾–2 inches long, and mostly smooth-margined. The petioles are very short. The flowers are clustered, white to greenish, and ⅙–⅓ inch long. The fruits are globose and dull blue when they mature in July, August, or September. These plants thrive on the slopes of eastern Oklahoma.

RABBITEYE BLUEBERRY

These shrubs are also known as Medium-cluster Blueberry. They are 1–3 feet tall and often are found in extensive colonies. The branches are slender, slightly hairy, and reddish to brown when mature. The leaves are simple, alternate, and narrowly oval with very short petioles. They are 1–2 inches long. The flowers are clustered on short stems, pink-tinged, and ⅙–¼ inch long. The fruits are globose, black when mature, lustrous, and ½–⅖ inch in diameter. They mature in July or August. These small shrubs are restricted to the pine-hickory forests of Oklahoma's southeastern counties (possibly only McCurtain County).

CHITTAMWOOD

These small trees are sometimes known as Wooly Buckthorn, Gum Elastic, and Wooly Bumelia. They grow to a height of 40 feet and have narrow crowns. The leaves are alternate, simple, obovate, entire, and 1–3 inches long. They have soft rust-colored hairs on the lower surfaces. The flowers are inconspicuous and white and grow in clusters. The fruits are drupes that are oblong, ½ inch long, black, shiny, and usually appear in clusters of 2–3. These plants are quite thorny and of very little benefit to people. They are widely distributed over the eastern two-thirds of Oklahoma, seem to thrive on well-drained slopes, and are especially abundant in oak-hickory associations.

PERSIMMON
Diospyros virginiana

Ebony Family
Ebenaceae

**COMMON
SWEETLEAF**
Symplocos tinctoria

Sweetleaf Family
Symplocaceae

FRINGE TREE
Chionanthus virginicus

Olive Family
Oleaceae

PERSIMMON

These trees are also known as Date Plum, Lotus Tree, Jove's Fruit, and Possumwood. They rarely exceed 50 feet in height with trunks of 1 foot in diameter. Typically the trunks are short and rather slender with rounded crowns. They frequently sprout from the roots and form thickets of small trees. They prefer well-drained, sandy loam soils and commonly occur in old fields or pastures. The leaves are simple, alternate, oval, pointed at the tips, entire, and 2–5 inches long. The fruits are spherical, about an inch thick, reddish yellow, and quite edible. They have several seeds which are dispersed by wildlife that feed on the pulpy fruit. These trees are common in all of Oklahoma except the far west.

COMMON SWEETLEAF

These trees are also known as Yellowwood and Horse Sugar. They are shrubby trees that are usually no more than 25 feet in height with a diameter of 6 inches. They grow in rich, moist soils, either in low places or on slopes. The leaves are simple, alternate, narrowly oval, pointed, slightly toothed, and 2–6 inches long. They have a sugary taste which contributes to two of their popular names. The small, creamy-white flowers are in compact clusters along the upper branches and emerge in early spring. The fruits, about ½ inch long, are orange-brown, ovoid, dry drupes. These trees are restricted to southeastern Oklahoma.

FRINGE TREE

These are large shrubs or small trees that are also known as Flowering Ash and Old Man's Beard. They often attain heights of 10–20 feet and rarely grow to be 40 feet tall. They prefer deep, moist soils along stream banks or borders of swamps. The leaves are simple, opposite, oval, entire, and 4–8 inches long. The petioles are stout and ½–1 inch long. The flowers are borne in loose, drooping panicles during May and June. Each flower has four white, long, slender petals which accounts for the name "Fringe Tree". The fruits are olive-like drupes that are ½–¾ inch long, dark bluish black, and mature in late fall. These shrubs occur in Oklahoma only in a few of the most southeastern counties.

DESERT OLIVE
Forestiera pubescens

Olive Family
Oleaceae

WHITE ASH
Fraxinus americana,
var. *americana*

Olive Family
Oleaceae

RED ASH
Fraxinus pennsylvanica

Olive Family
Oleaceae

DESERT OLIVE

These trees are sometimes known locally as Palo Blanco
and New Mexico Forestiera. They are usually only straggling
shrubs but in rare instances may reach heights of 40–50 feet
with trunks that are 5–6 inches thick. The leaves are simple,
opposite, oblong or oval, and ½–1¾ inches long. The
young twigs, as well as the leaves, are covered with gray
hairs. The fruits are ¼–⅓ inch long, oblong, and bluish
black when mature. These plants are found in moist, rich
soils of a few of Oklahoma's southwestern counties.

WHITE ASH

These trees are also known as American Ash, Cane Ash,
Biltmore Ash, and Biltmore White Ash. They grow to
heights of 100 feet or more with trunks that may be as
many as 3 feet thick. The leaves are opposite, pinnately
compound, and 8–13 inches long with 5–9 leaflets. The
leaflets are 2–4 inches long with serrate margins. The fruits
ripen in August or September. Their fruits are samaras in
6–8 inch clusters and each is 1–2½ inches long. These trees
are widely distributed in Oklahoma, especially in the eastern
portion. They seem to prefer low slopes and woodland
habitats.

RED ASH

These trees are also known as Green Ash, Blue Ash, and
Black Ash. They reach a height of 30–60 feet and branch
freely to form a broad crown. They occur in rich, moist soils
of lowlands and creek banks and only rarely ascend to
slopes of hillsides. The leaves are opposite and pinnately
compound with 5–9 leaflets. The leaflets are 2–6 inches
long and lancelike in form, with shallow-toothed margins
above the middle. The petioles are long, slender, and covered with short hairs. The fruits are 1–2 inches long with
narrow wings and are single-seeded samaras. These fruits
mature during the early fall but may remain attached until
the leaves are shed in late fall. These trees are distributed
over a large portion of Oklahoma.

PRIVET
Ligustrum vulgare

Olive Family
Oleaceae

BEAUTY BUSH
Callicarpa americana

Verbena Family
Verbenaceae

98

CATALPA
Catalpa speciosa

Trumpet Creeper Family
Bignoniaceae

PRIVET

These are shrubs that are also known as Prim, Primwort, Print, Skedge, and Skedgewith. They are profusely branched and 6–10 feet tall. They have escaped from cultivation and have become established along roadsides. They often grow in dense thickets when they find wet, rich, lowland meadows. The leaves are oblong to oval, obscurely veined, opposite in arrangement, simple, and 1–2 inches long. They usually remain attached to the stems through most of the winter. The flowers are white and about ¼ inch broad. The fruits are globular, black or blue, and about ¼ inch in diameter. These shrubs occur in southeastern Oklahoma.

BEAUTY BUSH

These are also known as French Mulberry, Bermuda Mulberry, and Sourbush. They are small shrubs that are seen only in the eastern half of Oklahoma and reach a height of some five feet. The stems are seldom branched above ground but grow in small clumps. They prefer moist open woods. The leaves are opposite, simple, ovate with sharp tips, toothed, and 3–6 inches long. The petioles are fairly short. The flowers are very small but appear in large, compact clusters on the upper nodes. The fruits mature in clusters that are quite striking. They are violet blue and each is globose with a diameter of ⅙–¼ inch. Attempts have been made to cultivate these shrubs, but it is difficult. They are widely distributed in eastern Oklahoma.

CATALPA

These trees are also known as Western Catalpa, Hardy Catalpa, and Bean Tree. They branch freely, have slow growth, and may reach a height of up to 100 feet and a trunk diameter of 3 feet. The leaves are opposite or in whorls of three, simple, heart-shaped, and 3–12 inches long. They have petioles that are slightly shorter than their blades. The flowers open in May or June and are white with some darker spots and 1–2 inches long. The fruits are 8 to 20-inch pods that are beanlike in structure but are actually capsules, not legumes. These trees are frequent in the low woodlands of most northeastern counties.

DESERT WILLOW
Chilopsis linearis

Trumpet Creeper Family
Bignoniaceae

BUTTONBUSH
Cephalanthus occidentalis

Madder Family
Rubiaceae

WHITE HONEYSUCKLE
Lonicera albiflora

Honeysuckle Family
Caprifoliaceae

DESERT WILLOW

These plants are sometimes known locally as Willowleaf Catalpa, Flowering Willow, and Flor de Mimbre. They are shrubs or small trees with slender, leaning trunks. The branches are weak and often droop at their tips in the manner of true willows. The leaves are opposite or alternate, linear to lanceolate in form, 3–8 inches long, and have smooth margins. The flowers are dark pink or purple and 1–1½ inches long. They are borne in panicles and are often very attractive during June and July. The fruits are slender capsules that are 4–12 inches long. These plants have been introduced, possibly as windbreaks, in several southwestern counties of Oklahoma. They seem to thrive in dry, sandy soils.

BUTTONBUSH

These trees are also known as Button Tree, Honey Ball, Globe Flower, Boxbush, Pinball, Snowball, Button Willow, Crane Willow, Swampwood, and River Bush. They are small freely branched trees that reach heights of 5–15 feet and are often very abundant along streams and lake-margins. The leaves are opposite (or whorled with 3 at each node), oval, entire-margined, and 3–6 inches long. The flowers and fruits are in globose clusters that are approximately an inch thick. The fruits become dry but are often retained intact into the late winter. They ultimately become reddish or brown. These small trees or shrubs are widely distributed where moist soils exist, but are less frequent in Oklahoma's westernmost counties.

WHITE HONEYSUCKLE

These plants are also known as Western Honeysuckle and Western White Honeysuckle. They are strongly branched shrubs that usually produce impenetrable clusters. They rarely develop into climbing vines. The leaves are simple, opposite, smooth, and broadly oval. The flowers appear in the spring and are white with a slight yellow tint. The fruits are globose berries that are ⅕–⅔ inch in diameter. They ripen in October or November. These plants grow along rocky ravines in a few southwestern counties.

AMERICAN ELDER
Sambucus canadensis

Honeysuckle Family
Caprifoliaceae

INDIAN CURRANT
Symphoricarpos orbiculatus

Honeysuckle Family
Caprifoliaceae

BLACK HAW
Viburnum prunifolium

Honeysuckle Family
Caprifoliaceae

AMERICAN ELDER

These are shrubs that are also known as Sweet Elder, Common Elder, Elder Blow, and Elderberry. They are 4–10 feet tall and not very woody. They have spreading, slender branches at the top which makes them domelike or flattened. They thrive in moist roadside drains or along streams. The leaves are pinnately compound with 5–11 leaflets. Each leaflet is 2–5 inches long, serrate, and sharply tipped. The flowers grow in loose clusters. They are white and very small. The fruits are globular, purple or black, about ¼ inch thick, and are attached by striking, red pedicels. They mature in September or October.

INDIAN CURRANT

These are small shrubs that are also known as Buckbrush, Buckbush, Turkeyberry, and Snapberry. They have underground runners which often spread over a wide area in leaf mold or sandy soil and form extensive thickets as undergrowth. Their choice habitat seems to be sandy or gravelly slopes where Post Oak trees abound. The stems are 2–5 feet tall. The leaves are 1–2 inches long, opposite, oval, and have even margins. The fruits are fleshy, several-seeded, ovoid to globose, and purple to red. They are ⅒–⅛ inch long and are clustered at the upper stem nodes. These little shrubs are widely distributed over Oklahoma and provide ground cover and food for many birds and mamals.

BLACK HAW

These trees are also known as Nannyberry, Stagbush, and Sheepberry. They are usually no taller than 15 feet but may sometimes reach a height of 25–30 feet. The trunks are 6–12 inches thick and typically crooked. The branches form low, broad, rounded crowns. They grow on dry, rocky hillsides and may form thickets along roadside fences. The leaves are simple and opposite with blades that are 1–3 inches long, oval, and serrate-margined. The fruits—borne in loose, terminal, red-stalked clusters—are oval, bright blue to black, and ½ inch long. They ripen in September and, if not consumed by birds, may remain attached until after leaf fall. These small trees occur only in eastern Oklahoma.

SAND SAGEBRUSH
Artemisia filifolia

Composite Family
Compositae

COTTONBUSH
Baccharis halimifolia

Composite Family
Compositae

WILLOW BACCHARIS
Baccharis salicina

Composite Family
Compositae

SAND SAGEBRUSH

These plants are also known as Wormwood. They are freely branched, aromatic shrubs that are usually less than 4 feet tall. The leaves are simple, alternate, sessile, 1–3 inches long, and very narrow. The entire plants are covered by silky gray hairs. The flowers and fruit are clustered along the upper branches and are not very conspicuous. These small shrubs are very numerous on sandy slopes of the western half of Oklahoma.

COTTONBUSH

These are shrubs that are also known as Groundsel Tree, Groundsel Bush, Pencil Tree, Cottonseed Tree, and Spikenard. They are freely branched, 3–10 feet tall, and thrive best in low, moist, rich, open meadows. The leaves are simple, alternate, obovate, coarsely toothed, and ½–3 inches long. The flowers are whitish to yellow and grow in compact heads at the tips of the numerous upper branches. The fruits are tiny achenes that mature in late autumn. They are striking because of their white capillary bristles that resemble cotton fibers. These little shrubs grow on the coastal plains of a few of Oklahoma's southeastern counties.

WILLOW BACCHARIS

These plants are also known as Western Baccharis. They are shrubs that are 3–6 feet tall and freely branched. The leaves are simple, alternate, 1–2 inches long, and slightly serrate on the margins. The flowers appear in May, June, or July and are in compact heads. The fruiting achenes are single-seeded. They mature in August and have a series of white bristles that aid in dispersal. These shrubs occur in Oklahoma only in the western half of the state.

References

Fernald, M. L. *Gray's Manual of Botany*. 8th ed. New York: American Book Co., 1950.

Gleason, H. A. *New Britton and Brown Illustrated Flora of the Northeastern States*. 3 vols. New York: New York Botanical Garden, 1952.

Goodman, George J. *Keys to the Spring Flora of Central Oklahoma*. Norman: University of Oklahoma Duplicating Service, 1960.

Grimm, William C. *Recognizing Native Shrubs*. Harrisburg, Pa.: Stackpole Co., 1966.

Lundell, C. L. *Flora of Texas*. 3 vols. Renner, Texas: Texas Research Foundation, 1961.

McCoy, Doyle. *A Study of Flowering Plants*. Lawton, Okla.: Cameron University Bookstore, 1976.

McCoy, Doyle. *Roadside Flowers of Oklahoma*. 2 vols. Lawton, Okla.: Cameron University Bookstore, 1976, 1978.

McCoy, Doyle. *Roadside Wild Fruits of Oklahoma*. Norman: University of Oklahoma Press, 1980.

Moore, Dwight M. *Trees of Arkansas*. Little Rock: Arkansas Forestry Commission, 1960.

Phillips, George R.; Gibbs, Frank J.; and Mattoon, Wilbur R. *Forest Trees of Oklahoma*. Oklahoma City: Forestry Division, State Board of Agriculture, 1959.

Preston, Richard J. *North American Trees*. 2d ed. Ames: Iowa State University Press, 1961.

Stemen, J. R.; and Myers, W. S. *Oklahoma Flora*. Oklahoma City: Harlow Publishing Co., 1937.

Steyermark, J. A. *Flora of Missouri*. Ames: Iowa State University Press, 1963.

Vines, Robert A. *Trees, Shrubs, and Woody Vines of the Southwest*. Austin: University of Texas Press, 1960.

Waterfall, U. T. *A Catalog of the Flora of Oklahoma*. Stillwater: Oklahoma State University Research Foundation, 1952.

Waterfall, U. T. *Keys to the Flora of Oklahoma*. 5th ed. Stillwater: Oklahoma State University Bookstore, 1960.

White, W. E. *Forest Trees of Texas*. College Station: Texas Forestry Association, 1946.

Williams, John E. *Atlas of the Woody Plants of Oklahoma*. Norman: Oklahoma Biological Survey, 1978.

Glossary

ACHENE.   A small, single-seeded, dry, unwinged fruit.

ACORN.   A nutlike fruit which is partly enclosed in a scale-covered cup. Commonly found on oaks.

ALTERNATE.   The arrangement on a stem of leaves, buds, and so forth, which are attached singly at each node.

AMENT.   A type of catkin.

ANTHER.   The pollen-bearing part of the stamen.

APEX.   The tip of a leaf, stem, etc.

AXIL.   The upper angle between a leaf or other structure and the axis from which it originates.

AXILLARY.   Situated in an axil.

BARK.   The outer covering of trunks or branches of trees.

BASE.   The bottom of a leaf blade.

BERRY.   A fruit that is fleshy or pulpy throughout.

BLADE.   The broad, flat portion of a leaf.

BLOOM.   The powdery, whitish or bluish substance on certain leaves that may be rubbed off.

BRACT.   A modified (reduced) leaf usually located at the base of a flower or flower cluster.

BUD.   An undeveloped branch or flower.

BUR.   A dry fruit covered with spines.

CAPSULE.   Dry fruit that splits to release seeds from one or more compartments.

CATKIN.   Cylindrical cluster of male or female flowers.

CHAMBERED.   Pith with cross-partitions.

COMPOUND.   Composed of two or more parts, as a leaf that contains leaflets.

CROWN.   The upper part of a tree with its branches and leaves.

CUP. Bowllike or cuplike structure that contains the nuts of oaks, and similar trees or shrubs.

DECIDUOUS. Falling away, as leaves of many trees do in the autumn.

DEHISCENT. Splitting open.

DELTOID. Broadly triangular in form; resembling a river delta.

DIVERGENT. Spreading, such as leaves or buds; pointing outward from the stem.

DOUBLY-TOOTHED. Descriptive of a leaf margin, such as that of an elm leaf, where the larger teeth have smaller teeth on them.

DOWNY. Covered by soft hairs.

DRUPE. A type of fruit, such as that of the plum, where the fleshy outer portion surrounds a hard inner layer which, in turn, encloses a single seed.

ELLIPTIC. Egglike, with rounded ends.

ENTIRE. A leaf that has smooth margins (no teeth, etc.)

EVERGREEN. Trees whose leaves remain attached and green during winter seasons.

FILAMENT. The stalk of a stamen which supports an anther.

FLAKY. Used to apply to bark that peels off.

FLESHY. Juicy or succulent.

FOLIACEOUS. Leafy or leaflike.

FOLIAGE. The leaves.

FOLLICLE. A fruiting pod that splits along one side only.

FRUIT. A ripened ovary; the seed-bearing portion of a plant.

GLAND. A secreting structure that is usually imbedded, at least partly, within the surface of a leaf, etc.

GLOBULAR. Spherical or nearly spherical in shape.

GYMNOSPERM. A tree, such as the pine, that bears naked seeds on the tops of cone scales.

HABIT. General appearance.

HABITAT. Location where a plant grows naturally, such as a rocky slope, etc.

HEAD. The crown of a tree.

HOARY. Having gray or whitish leaves.

HYBRID. A plant that is produced as a result of a cross between two somewhat different plants.

INDEHISCENT. Nonsplitting, as in nuts.

INFLORESCENCE. The manner in which flowers are arranged on an axis.

109

INVOLUCRE. Collection of floral bracts.

JOINT. Stem portion where leaves attach; node.

LANCEOLATE. A leaf that is broadest near the base and tapers to a pointed tip; lance-shaped.

LEAVES. The variously shaped structures on the twigs of trees. They may be joined to the stem by stalks (petioles) or be stalkless (sessile). Their blades may be flattened or cylindrical. The blades may be in single (one-leaf) units or in separate (compound) units.

LEAFLET. A single unit of a compound leaf.

LEAF SCAR. A scar indicating the point where a leaf petiole was attached before leaf fall.

LEGUME. A podlike fruit that usually splits along two sides when mature.

LENTICEL. A corky spot on a young, woody stem.

LINEAR. Referring to a long, slender structure.

LOBE. Rounded segment on the margin of a leaf or other structure.

LUSTROUS. Shiny or glossy.

MARGIN. Edge of a leaf or other structure.

MIDRIB. The mid-vein of a leaf.

NEEDLE. A very narrow leaf such as that of a pine.

NODE. The place on a stem where leaves are attached.

NUT. A hard-coated, single-seeded, dry fruit.

NUTLET. A very small nut.

OBOVATE. Egg-shaped, with the widest portion near the apex.

OPPOSITE. Leaves, buds, etc., which are paired on opposite sides of the same node.

OVAL. Egg-shaped, with the widest point at about the mid-point between the base and the apex.

OVARY. The fruiting portion of flowers.

OVATE. Egg-shaped, with the widest portion near the base.

OVULE. The part of the ovary that is a potential seed.

PALMATE. The arrangement of parts which arise from approximately the same point and spread outward.

PANICLE. A loose, branched inflorescence.

PEDICEL. Stalk of an individual flower or fruit.

PETIOLE. Leaf stalk.

PINNATE. Featherlike arrangement of veins or leaflets.

PINNATELY COMPOUND. A compound leaf on which the leaflets are attached to a central rachis.

PITH. The soft, central portion of a stem.

POD. Any dry, splitting fruit.

POME. A fleshy fruit such as the apple, in which the receptacle surrounds the ovary and becomes a part of the fruit.

PRICKLE. A type of spine that is small but sharp.

RACHIS. The central stalk of a pinnately compound leaf to which leaflets attach laterally.

RESINOUS. Covered with gummy substance.

SAMARA. A single-seeded, nonsplitting, winged fruit, such as those of elm and maple trees.

SCALE. A thin, dry, membrane, such as the covering on winter buds.

SCURF. A small, irregular scale.

SEED. A ripened ovule.

SERRATE. Saw-toothed.

SESSILE. Stalkless as in a leaf that lacks a petiole.

SHRUB. Low, woody plant.

SIMPLE. One segment or one piece.

SINUATE. Wavy margin or surface.

SINUS. Recess between two lobes.

SPIKE. Sessile flowers on a common stem.

STAMEN. The male organ of a flower, composed of an anther and a filament.

STIPULE. A leaflike appendage at the base of a leaf petiole; usually paired.

SUTURE. Seamlike line of splitting on a dry fruit.

TRUNK. The main stem of a tree.

TWIG. A young shoot.

UMBEL. A type of floral arrangement with several pedicels attached at the tip of a single stem.

UNISEXUAL. Plants that have the stamens and pistil or pistils on separate flowers.

VEIN. A vascular bundle in a leaf.

VISCID. Covered with sticky substance.

WHORL. A cycle of three or more leaves attached to the same node on the stem.

Index

112

114

115

116